Vocational Education

in

America's Schools

Major Issues of the 1970's

Gerald B. Leighbody

Emeritus Professor of Education State University of New York Buffalo, New York

AMERICAN TECHNICAL SOCIETY

CHICAGO 60637

PREFACE

It is the purpose of this book to identify and examine the major issues presently facing American education and its leaders regarding the role and nature of occupational education in the nation's schools. By definition, an issue is an unresolved question, subject to differing points of view and therefore under debate. There are many such issues involved in determining the place which vocational or occupational education should occupy in the American educational scheme. Those which have been selected for inclusion here are the ones which appear to be central to the entire vocational education enterprise. On these issues the educational planners are forced to take a position in order to act, and the decisions they make reflect the views they hold. Unfortunately, educational decisions of great consequence are sometimes made without full awareness by the decision makers of the issues involved or of the assumptions accepted concerning them.

No attempt will be made to resolve fully the issues which are discussed. Most of them are open-ended in the sense that new knowledge often modifies the views of thoughtful people, and new knowledge about these particular issues continues to be forthcoming through research, study and experience. The effort, therefore, will be to inquire into the leading viewpoints and positions relating to each issue and to examine the most relevant research, scholarly thinking and other evidence relating to it.

As a matter of organization, and to aid in orderly discussion, each of the major issues is treated in a separate chapter. It quickly becomes apparent, however, that most, if not all of them, are interrelated, and in considering any of the issues selected, aspects of others become involved. These relationships will be pointed out when they occur.

The terms vocational education and occupational education are used interchangeably and are intended to mean the same thing. Occupational education can properly include baccalaureate and graduate studies in colleges and universities which prepare for professional and similar careers, but the problems of vocational education at these levels are not the subject of this volume. Rather, it is concerned with the critical questions about vocational education which arise at the levels of the elementary, secondary and the two-year post secondary schools.

Largely because of the unusual amount of vocational and manpower legislation enacted by the Congress since 1960, the movement presently finds itself in a period of rapid growth, with new and added responsibilities and much encouraging support. At the same time there is a good deal of skepticism about many current practices and trends, much sharp scrutiny, and a new insistence upon frequent and careful evaluation of results. There is much justified enthusiasm and hope for the future, accompanied by considerable turmoil, questioning and uncertainty. It is pre-eminently a time for a critical review of many basic assumptions and issues, so that as the program gains wider acceptance its growth can be built upon sound and lasting foundations. It is hoped that this book may contribute to this end.

For the experiences which made possible the writing of this book, I am deeply indebted to my teachers and to my colleagues in the vocational education movement. I am equally indebted to my students for the encouragement to undertake and to complete the task. To all of them, past and present, this book is dedicated.

GERALD B. LEIGHBODY

CONTENTS

CHAPTER 1

THE GOALS OF VOCATIONAL EDUCATION

The Need to Consider Goals

Any discussion of the problems which confront present day educational leaders with respect to vocational education quickly leads to the question of its goals. What are the goals of vocational education? What role is it expected to play in the system of American education? There is disagreement as to what these goals are and what they ought to be. There are certain goals of vocational education which are widely accepted by vocational educators, but are questioned by other educators. There are goals which are emphasized by some vocational educators and played down by others. And there are goals which some consider quite appropriate at certain educational levels, but not at others. Most of the issues which arise in practice emerge from these disagreements, for as goals differ so do philosophies and methods. Views which are adopted, and evidence supporting them, become more or less germane and carry more or less weight depending upon what goals one accepts for vocational education and expects it to achieve.

Further, the goals of vocational education in American schools have important historical antecedents and to understand them in their present form calls for some understanding of their historical development. A depth study of this historical background would not be consistent with the purposes of this book, but the review presented in this chapter should be a sufficient historical basis for the discussions which follow.

There is an additional reason why an examination of the goals of vocational education is especially timely. Evaluation of program results has always been considered important, but the latest vocational legislation requires an annual assessment of vocational education, state by state and in national terms, and places the responsibility for this evaluation upon state and national advisory councils created for this purpose.[1] (Numbers correspond to the list of references following each chapter.) It is a well known principle of program evaluation that the measurement of achivement must be based upon the goals which were intended. It is essential, then, for some agreement to be reached upon the goals of vocational education, and to have them understood by those who will be judging the effectiveness of the program.

Some Early Influences

Vocational education in the public schools has been the subject of educational debate in America for at least one hundred years. The Morrill Act of 1862, an act of Congress, placed the national government and the states in support of publicly financed education designed to train youth in the two kinds of occupations which predominated at that time—agriculture and industry. From that time until the present the fortunes of vocational education have been identified with specific federal legislation to a greater extent than any other aspect of American education.[2]

It may be argued that these laws have themselves established the goals of vocational education. Yet one must look behind the laws to know why and how they reached their final form. Laws are but the expression of public policies which reflect, under our system, the purposes which have popular support at the time they are enacted. Laws relating to vocational education, like most others, have been shaped by many forces, and especially by individuals whose leadership and capacity to articulate their views were most influential at the time the laws were drafted. The philosophies of these leaders and the goals they have espoused account for the provisions of the controlling legislation. To understand the origin of many of the present concepts of vocational education it is most helpful to look to the writings of those who led the movement during its formative period.

The effect of the Morrill Act was to create institutions which later became the land grant colleges in most states and ultimately, in many cases, the present state universities. Their programs of vocational education have emerged as advanced professional schools, chiefly in agriculture and engineering. The development of these schools was not without controversy as to their objectives, but they have now achieved an accepted and acceptable role in the area of higher education and their purpose has ceased to be the subject of much debate. Once it became clear, however, that they would not engage in training workers for occupations of less than professional status, calls were heard for some type of education to serve those who would become farmers, artisans, and other skilled workers. These programs were seen as belonging in the lower schools and it is here that the collision of viewpoints regarding the goals of vocational education chiefly occurs.

More Recent Influences

Powerful social forces have brought vocational education under more widespread and critical scrutiny during the past decade than at any other time since 1917. Within a period of ten years three Presidents have appointed or worked with citizens' commissions created to study the national program of vocational education and to make recommendations for its modernization and improvement. Each of these groups has produced a significant report. The Panel of Consultants on Vocational Education appointed in 1961 by President Kennedy presented a major report entitled *Education For a Changing World of Work*. This led to the passage by Congress of the Vocational Education Act of 1963. As required by this Act, President Johnson appointed the Advisory Council on Vocational Education in 1967. Its report, *The Bridge Between Man and His Work*, resulted in substantial revision of the 1963 Act in the form of the Vocational Education Amendments Act of 1968. This 1968 law required the creation of a continuing National Advisory Council on Vocational Education, which began to function in 1969. The first report of this Council was submitted to President Nixon and the Congress in the same year, and contained important findings and recommendations. The Council, with its counterpart in each state, will regularly monitor and evaluate the program in the future. The

Educational Compact of the States, an organization of leading educators and political leaders devoted to the improvement of American education, has placed vocational education high on its list of priority concerns. Since 1960 the educational literature has been replete with discussions of the subject, including notable contributions by Conant.[3, 4] Major professional journals have published entire issues dealing with the problems of vocational education.[5, 6] Foundations, such as Ford and Upjohn have allocated funds and personnel to the improvement of vocational education. Any number of national and regional conferences have been held to consider the effects of the new legislation and the reports of the various commissions.[7, 8, 9] In no other decade in America has vocational education received as much official attention as in the last.

Many of the reports, articles and conferences have been critical of the traditional approaches to vocational education and not a few respected voices have called for fundamental changes. Others believe that few, if any, changes are necessary except for better funding and wider acceptance of the program. Under conditions of such interest and concern the goals of vocational education and their justification become the starting place for any examination of the issues involved.

The Basic Justifications for Vocational Education

As we have seen, disappointment over the failure of the land grant colleges to train workers for farm and factory led to growing demands for some other means to accomplish this. By the early part of the present century several groups with an interest in such training had formed a working coalition, and in 1917 were able to secure the enactment of the Smith-Hughes law, which promoted and financed vocational education of less than college grade in the public school system of the nation.[10] This law had several features which permitted it to determine the purposes and nature of vocational education in these schools for nearly fifty years thereafter. Its passage was preceded by several years of effort to convince the Congress of the importance of and need for such a program, and during this period the arguments put forth to justify vocational education appeared in their clearest form. Many of the arguments have their proponents today, and now, as then, others tend to question their validity.

There were three main lines of argument used by the advocates of vocational education in claiming a place for it in American education. Briefly stated they can be classified as the philosophical, the economic, and the sociological.[11]

The Philosophical Positions

Many of those who led the fight for the introduction of vocational education into the school curriculum did so because of a strong philosophical commitment to equality of educational opportunity. They believed that the high school at that time was concerned only with the needs of youth who were preparing for college. Because education beyond the high school was pursued by a very small minority of college age youth, the college preparation emphasis was held to be undemocratic, and unfair to the great majority of young people, most of whom never finished high school.[12] This same position is often taken by vocational leaders today, although at present nearly fifty percent of all youth continue their education beyond high school. Those who, in 1917, spoke for vocational education maintained that the schools had an obligation to serve those who moved from the high school into the world of work, as well as those who moved on to college, and that vocational education should therefore be provided as an alternative to college preparation. Few opposed the belief in equal opportunity for all, but some questioned the idea that vocational education was the only, or even the best, curricular alternative to preparation for college.

Resting the argument on democratic grounds introduced another issue which tended to confuse the discussion and the thinking—the controversy of liberal vs utilitarian education. Early spokesmen for vocational education defined the general education offerings of the high schools and the colleges as liberal education, and they further considered the liberal studies to be education for an aristocratic elite and education for leisure.[13] They insisted that this was contrary to the spirit of American democracy and to the American way of life and that vocational education was needed as a form of utilitarian education for the masses to counterbalance the overemphasis upon liberal education for the elite. This distrust of liberal education by vocational educators has never been fully overcome, and attitudes ranging from suspicion to near hostility toward liberal education can still be found among some vocational education leaders. The roots of some of the most difficult of the current problems can be traced back to these early attitudes. They will be explored more fully in the chapter which follows.

The Economic Argument

Much of the attention of those who founded vocational education was directed to its economic benefits. By 1900 the nation was beginning to feel the effects of a diminished supply of skilled workers because of a reduction in the stream of immigrants from Europe with a background in the skilled occupations. America had developed no adequate apprenticeship system for training such workers, and vocational education was looked upon by many as a substitute for apprenticeship.[14] At the same time the first advances in scientific agriculture were beginning to flow from the research and experimentation carried on at the land grant colleges, but better educated farmers were needed to take advantage of them. It was claimed, therefore, that since the two largest segments of the economy, industry and agriculture, stood in need of better trained workers, the schools should contribute to the economic welfare of the country by helping to provide them through vocational training.

Agricultural and industrial interests were not alone in their efforts to persuade the schools to accept the preparation of trained workers as a goal. Business leaders were dissatisfied because the high schools were not training enough young people for the growing number of office and clerical jobs.[15] Even before 1900 many high schools had introduced commercial courses, and indeed it may be said that business education was the first form of vocational education to appear in the American high school. Before 1895 the NEA had organized a Department of Business Education, as well as a Department of Industrial Education and Manual Training. Yet the business community was not much pleased with the work being done in the high school commercial courses because the graduates did not meet its employment standards.[16]

This was an early expression of one concept of the purpose of vocational education which has persisted down to the present time and which is still uppermost in the thinking of many of its sponsors. It is the belief that vocational education is designed to meet the employment needs of particular areas of the economy, and of particular occupations within those areas. It leads to the assumption on the part of many employers and vocational educators that the training provided should be so closely matched with specific job requirements as to permit immediate productive performance by the trainee in an entry job. This expectation is implicit in the Smith-Hughes law and in all subsequent legislation prior to the Vocational Education Act of 1963. Yet as long ago as 1927 Mays had questioned the merit of this goal and had demonstrated on practical grounds the futility of trying to achieve it.[17]

The Vocational Education Act of 1963 did not reject the goal of meeting the nation's economic needs but it turned the emphasis of the program toward meeting the needs of people. It assumed that vocational education's primary objective is to help people of all employable age groups and every category of need to become and remain gainfully employed. This would, of course, satisfy the need for trained workers, but the change in emphasis is nevertheless significant. It reorients vocational education to more sociological and humanitarian goals.

The Sociological Argument

From the beginning, sociological and humanistic reasons have been used to justify the need for vocational education. From one point of view this may also have an economic component, for it can be argued that those who are trained for a job, and so become wage earners, will thereby turn out to be more useful and contributing citizens who will be assets to society rather than dependents. Thus, by performing its primary function of preparation for useful employment, vocational education is thought to contribute indirectly to many other social benefits.

Among those who became interested in vocational education in its early days there was a strong element of philanthropic and social welfare thinking, and the general uplifting of the masses through training for work was thought by many to be an attainable goal. Evidence that this idea still persists is to be found in the number and variety of job training programs which have been undertaken by government in recent years as a part of the war on poverty, in the hope of improving the lot of the deprived and the disadvantaged. A number of social reformers and professional sociologists, such as David Snedden, were among those who contributed extensively to the philosophy and the literature of vocational education. Some writers have been so convinced of the broad social value of vocational education that they have suggested that it can be somewhat of a social panacea. Prosser and Allen in *Vocational Education in a Democracy,* published in 1925, ascribed most social ills to vocational incompetence and therefore concluded that vocational education was the answer to many of them. Among those they mentioned were unemployment, the alienation of youth, lack of respect for American institutions, juvenile delinquency, adult crime and unstable and unsatisfactory homes. Indeed, they perceived vocational education as nothing less than the salvation of civilization. While, in retrospect, these may seem like somewhat extravagant and grandiose claims, the July 15, 1969 report of the National Council on Vocational Education places equal faith in the capacity of vocational education to solve the major social problems of our time. Like Prosser and Allen, the authors of this report attribute the existence of these problems entirely to unemployment, particularly youth unemployment. On the grounds that more vocational education would reduce or eliminate much of this unemployment, they believe that it would also reduce violence, distrust of society by the young, campus and inner city revolt, and racial unrest.

Vocational Education and Social Class

Other sociological concerns have played a part in forming the rationale which supports vocational education, and have generated some of its most persistent problems. These have to do with the question of social stratification. As we have seen, the American high school was regarded for many years by its critics as being too completely devoted to college preparation. It is still subject to this criticism. But beyond this, the college was thought of as the training ground for society's leaders. On the other hand the high school came to be considered the school which offered education for the masses. It was expected to be terminal for all but a few students, as in fact it was, and was referred to by some writers as the people's college. If vocational education was indeed to become the alternative to college preparatory studies, the emergence of two kinds of education, one for leaders and one workers, became a possibility. The problem was further confused by the growing tendency by some reformers to consider the academic subjects as having little or no value except to meet the requirements for college entrance. This reaction against academic learning has been characteristic of some vocational leaders and while it is not necessarily a form of anti-intellectualism, to some critics of vocational education it appears to be. At any rate, it has helped to influence vocational education toward a more narrow and utilitarian role than many thoughtful educators feel they can accept.

To them it has seemed that there is a real danger in this approach, the danger of an educational dualism based on social class which, if widely accepted, might tend to strengthen social stratification. This fear, as much as anything else, accounted for the opposition of John Dewey and others to vocational education so long as it stressed primarily job training. This problem has continued to trouble many observers and students of vocational education and the difficult issue of separatism is still before us. The possibility of creating a type of caste system in the American society through a dualistic educational process was debated during the discussions which led to the adoption of the Smith-Hughes law and there were some who did not hesitate to promote vocational education on the basis of social and economic class distinctions. Robert Thurston, a prominent advocate of trade training in the schools, in a paper delivered at the NEA in 1893, stated that the trade school should become the high school for those who could not afford college.[18]

Thurston clearly viewed vocational education as the appropriate form of education for the lower classes. Others, in one way or another, have shared this belief although they may not recognize that their attitudes are related to social class. The first report of the recently created National Advisory Council on Vocational Education, issued in July 1969, says that the majority of Americans feel that vocational education is designed for somebody else's children and accuses the nation of being guilty of intellectual snobbery where vocational education is concerned. Clearly, in the minds of some, the goal of vocational education is to meet the needs of those who are less fortunate economically, socially and intellectually.

The European Influence

The thinking which favored a form of educational dualism was supported during the early 1900s by some industrial and educational leaders who greatly admired the systems for training workers which had developed in western Europe. They were especially enamored of the German model, which was held to be the most efficient means for assuring a constant and adequate supply of skilled workers in an industrial nation. In Germany all children received a common basic education, designed to impart basic literacy and civic competence. At that point those who were to become the future leaders were identified from the future workers and from then on the two groups pursued quite different educational paths. Those destined for leadership roles followed a rigid and demanding academic program leading to higher schools and to the university. The great majority (ninety percent) became learners or apprentices in the many industries, businesses, and other enterprises of the nation, under a well planned program in which the schools provided some part time instruction related to the learners' fields of work. In determining the future economic and social status of the individual, and therefore the kind of education he would receive, intellectual and other forms of potential were claimed to be the major criterions, but in reality social class and family status and prestige played a very important part. This approach to education helped to perpetuate in Germany a social caste system which was quite in contrast to the open and fluid social movement which was prized, if not always achieved, by most Americans. The thought of one kind of education for leaders and a different kind for workers was repugnant to the spirit of egalitarianism which had become part of the American tradition. It seemed to many to deny the principle of equal opportunity for all. Therefore, efficient or not, Americans were not disposed to accept any such arrangement.[19] Organized labor, in particular, was strongly opposed to it, for the working man feared that it would be his children who would be chiefly enrolled in vocational courses, and he felt that they should have the same opportunity as others to climb the economic and social ladder through education. As a result, labor withheld its support of federal vocational legislation until it was assured that the program would avoid the dualistic approach.

The Manual Training Influence

The introduction of the manual arts into the elementary and secondary school curriculum began late in the nineteenth century and this movement became involved with the goals of vocational education. Over the years it has evolved into the present program of industrial arts. Perhaps the best known educator to be associated with the manual arts idea in its early days was Calvin Woodward of St. Louis, although many others, including John Dewey approved and supported the concept.[20] Like many other educational innovations the aims of manual training, as it came to be known, were perceived differently by different thinkers and misunderstood by many. Some saw it as a means for making traditional subjects more practical. Others claimed that it served as pre-vocational education in supplying general vocational preparation, principally for the artisan occupations, by teaching skills common to many of them.[21] This did not satisfy those who were promoting vocational education, while, at the same time, Woodward, Dewey and others who were opposed to specialized vocational education did their best to disassociate the manual arts program from programs of trade training. They felt that it was not intended as preparation for skilled work or any other type of occupation. On the other hand, those most interested in vocational education insisted that to be vocational the curriculum must include training that leads directly to a specific and recognized occupation.

As a result, present-day industrial arts and other practical arts make use of shop and laboratory experiences chiefly to help students achieve technological literacy through an understanding of the major technological and economic processes of a highly industrialized society. It is only fair to say, however, that the distinctions between the practical arts and vocational education which seem so clear to the leaders in both fields are, even today, far from clear in the minds of many educators and other citizens.

Vocational Education and Work Orientation

Vocational educators have always believed that to be successful they must have the privilege of selecting for their courses the students who can best profit by the instruction and who are most likely to succeed in the occupation for which they prepare. Thus the question of predicting occupational suitability and the process of making a good occupational choice become matters of great importance. Clearly, this involves the field of vocational guidance, and vocational education has had a long, and not always harmonious relationship with the guidance movement.

There has been a good deal of ambivalence on the part of vocational educators as to the kind and amount of responsibility they should assume in the area of vocational guidance. On the one hand they have often been critical of professional guidance personnel for what they consider to be poor vocational counseling. They complain that many counselors direct students mainly toward college careers and too often discourage able students from choosing vocational courses, urging only the academically weak students to enroll in them. Yet there have been few attempts by vocational educators to take an active part in the guidance function through pre-vocational and exploratory or tryout activities. Beginning with the George-Barden law[22] of 1946 federal vocational funds have been available for vocational guidance purposes, and this encouragement was strengthened in the Vocational Education Acts of 1963 and 1968. Nevertheless, vocational education leadership has been reluctant to assume any great responsibility for work orientation as a part of its program. The *American Vocational Journal*, the publication of the American Vocational Association, is probably the most authoritative and responsible voice now speaking for vocational education. An editorial in a recent issue discusses the question of using the funds available from federal sources for career guidance and work orientation. It acknowledges the great need for occupational orientation by all young people, and then goes on to say that vocational and technical education is for those who are preparing to enter the labor market, and that too much emphasis upon activities such as vocational orientation could interfere with this primary goal.[23] Work experience programs have been used effectively for occupational orientation and exploration, but the same editorial makes it clear that, while vocational guidance and orientation are needed and useful, they are not a legitimate function of vocational education. Only when a given occupation has been chosen does vocational education begin to serve the student.

Vocational Education and School Holding Power

It has often been suggested that vocational education can be the means for capturing and holding the interest of many high school students who find that the more academic studies are not to their liking or aptitude and that enrollment in vocational courses will encourage them to stay in school rather than become dropouts. Another theory is that students who dislike the academic subjects and do poorly in them may find them more meaningful and interesting if they are taking a vocational program and if these subjects can be taught as applied to their occupational interests. Vocational educators have at times mentioned both of these goals as among the desirable outcomes of vocational education. However, the practice of using vocationally related activities as a method for stimulating better attitudes toward general studies has been so limited that the evidence concerning its success is very meager, and no research has been done which would produce any real answers about this question. Some studies have been made of the comparative dropout rates among high school students enrolled in vocational programs and those in other types of programs. These have been mostly in the form of local, informal studies, in scattered areas of the country, and they show no significant differences in the dropout rates between the two groups. In some large cities, however, dropouts from vocational courses substantially exceed those from the more general curriculum. Most vocational educators do not feel that vocational education should be promoted on the basis of its appeal to the wavering student or the student who lacks academic aptitude.

Vocational Education Beyond the High School

Quite recently there have been recommendations that question the high school as the appropriate place for the development of specific vocational competence. In the light of the rapid increase in the numbers of youth who are extending their education beyond high school and in consideration of several other trends, suggestions are frequently made that the objectives of high school vocational education should no longer include specialized preparation for a particular occupation. Such preparation would be expected in programs immediately following the completion of high school. One of the strongest statements to this effect is contained in a report of a study on Vocational, Occupational and Technical Education conducted during the summer of 1965 at the Massachusetts Institute of Technology, sponsored by the United States Office of Education. Nearly 150 persons from education, industry, business, government and the sciences participated in the conferences which produced the report. The report recommends strongly against specific vocational training in the high school.[24]

A good many vocational educators are not yet ready to accept this recommendation. They point to the twenty-five percent of the youth group who still fail to complete high school and the additional numbers for whom the high school is still terminal, to support their belief that there is still need for specific occupational preparation for many high school students. The strong trend toward some kind of formal post high school education for more and more young people will make this whole question a matter of continuing debate during the years to come, and the issue will be discussed more fully in a later chapter.

On-The-Job Training

Some educators, economists and others believe that vocational education would be more effective if it was limited largely to supplementing on-the-job training rather than engaging in pre-employment training. They cite the vast number of different occupations in which people are employed and indicate that most of them can be learned only through on-the-job experience and training. They would recommend that the schools emphasize general work orientation, career decision making, and the sharpening of those fundamental academic skills which are required in most jobs, leaving particular job skills to be learned after employment. They feel that vocational education is most effective when offered for adults who are already employed so that they may improve their skills or learn new skills when needed for job survival or change.[25]

Most vocational educators question this viewpoint. They agree that the needs of employed adults are important and should be served, and they call attention to the large amount of upgrading and supplementary education for employed persons which has been characteristic of vocational programs. But they also believe that pre-employment training is essential for many young people because of the increasing difficulty experienced by many of them in finding meaningful employment.

Job Placement as a Goal

Vocational educators are nearly unanimous in accepting job placement as a responsibility, and the placement of graduates in the occupations for which they were trained has always been considered the most tangible measure of the success of the vocational educational process. As recently as 1962 the report of the Panel of Consultants on Vocational Education stated, "The acid test of vocational education is the extent to which its graduates are employed in the occupations for which they are trained."[26]

Summary

Without question, the fundamental goal of vocational education which is most widely accepted by its leaders is to prepare people to enter into and remain in gainful employment. They further believe that to achieve this goal requires that each student be instructed specifically in the job skills and technical knowledge demanded by the occupation he has chosen.

It is believed that by accomplishing this primary goal, several other valuable outcomes will be realized, and that these may also be included as goals of vocational education. Among them are:

1. The nation will be provided with the trained workers needed to maintain its economic health and growth.
2. Unemployment and underemployment caused by lack of training and education will be reduced or eliminated.
3. Many other social evils associated with unemployment and economic deprivation will be diminished.
4. Individuals will benefit by becoming productive and contributing members of society rather than its dependents, and that many personal as well as social gains will result.
5. The educational system will be more democratic because it will offer equal opportunities and benefits to all, rather

than bestowing most of its rewards upon the academically talented.

6. Students who have little interest in formal academic subjects may find these subjects more meaningful when they are taught in relation to occupational goals, and this may encourage them to continue their education.

The orientation of youth to the world of work is recognized as being essential to the process of occupational choice, and ultimately to the success of any program of occupational preparation. However, there is not complete agreement upon the kind and amount of responsibility for work orientation which should be assumed by vocational education as contrasted with the function of specific job training.

There are many who question whether the commitment to training for specific occupations is any longer an appropriate goal for the high school, although they believe it to be a legitimate and necessary goal of post high school occupational education.

Some believe that vocational education should strive for a generalized preparation for broad occupational clusters, depending upon on-the-job experience to teach the skills of particular jobs. Others see no merit in this approach, and consider it to be a watered down, ineffective kind of vocational education. The question of which occupational skills should be taught in schools and which should be employment based remains largely unresolved.

Since 1946, and with increasing public support, the nation has committed itself to the maintenance of full employment, to the elimination of poverty, and to the uplifting of the economic status of those who have not shared in the general affluence. Vocational education has come to be looked upon as one of the means of economic and social rehabilitation for the less fortunate in our society, and it has become a matter of public policy that this shall be one of its goals.

Employment of the vocational graduate in the occupation for which he has prepared is accepted by all vocational educators.

REFERENCES

(References correspond to numbered items in the text)

1. U. S. Congress. *Vocational Education Amendments Act.* Public Law 90-576, 90th Cong., 1968.
2. Leighbody, Gerald. *Organization and Operation of a Local Program of Vocational Education,* Chapter 3. Washington: United States Office of Education, 1968.
3. Conant, James B. *The American High School Today.* New York: McGraw-Hill Co., 1959.
4. Conant, James B. *The Comprehensive High School.* New York: McGraw-Hill Co., 1967.
5. *Phi Delta Kappan,* no. 46 (April, 1965).
6. *Bulletin of the National Association of Secondary Principals* 49, no. 301 (May, 1965).
7. Massachusetts Institute of Technology. *Final Report of the Summer Study on Occupational, Vocational and Technical Education.* Cambridge, Mass.: Massachusetts Institute of Technology, 1965.
8. Aerospace Education Foundation and the United States Office of Education. National Conference on Educating for the World of Work (January, 1970).
9. *National Conference on the Need for a Renewed Conception of Vocational and Technical Education.* Columbia University, 1965.
10. Swanson, Chester J. *Developments of Federal Legislation for Vocational Education.* Chicago: American Technical Society, 1962.
11. Fisher, Berenice M. *Industrial Education: American Ideals and Institutions.* Madison: University of Wisconsin Press, 1967.
12. Prosser, Charles A. and Quigley, Thomas H. *Vocational Education in a Democracy.* Chicago: American Technical Society, 1949.
13. Ibid., Chapter 2.
14. Mays, Arthur B. *The Problem of Industrial Education.* New York: The Century Co., 1927.
15. Fisher. *Industrial Education: American Ideals and Institutions.*
16. Ibid.
17. Mays. *The Problem of Industrial Education.*
18. Fisher. *Industrial Education: American Ideals and Institutions.*
19. Mays. *The Problem of Industrial Education.*
20. Dewey, John. *The School and Society.* Chicago: University of Chicago Press, 1899.
21. Mays, Arthur B. *Principles and Practices of Vocational Education.* New York: McGraw-Hill Co., 1948.
22. U. S. Congress. *The George-Barden Act.* Public Law 586, 79th Cong., 1946.
23. Burkett, Lowell A. "Latest Word from Washington." *American Vocational Journal* 44, no. 1 (January, 1969): 5-6.
24. Massachusetts Institute of Technology. *Report of the Summer Study on Occupational, Vocational and Technical Education.*
25. Ginzberg, Eli, and Hiestland, Dale. *New Conceptions of Vocational and Technical Education,* edited by J. Rosenberg. New York: Teachers College Press, 1967.
26. Panel of Consultants on Vocational Education. *Education for a Changing World.* Washington, D. C.: United States Government Printing Office, 1962.

CHAPTER 2

SEPARATISM OR MERGER FOR VOCATIONAL EDUCATION?

Historical Reasons for Separatism

Many vocationalists have believed that in the field of vocational education the problems of administration and supervision are totally different from those in general education.

Such a statement was made by two of the most influential pioneer leaders of the vocational education movement, John C. Wright and Charles R. Allen, in a book which appeared in 1926, and is a forceful expression of a conviction shared by many vocational educators before and since that time.[1] Wright became the Director of the Federal Board for Vocational Education, and later Assistant Commissioner for Vocational Education in the United States Office of Education. Allen was a consultant to the Federal Board and a prominent writer and leader in the field of vocational education for many years.

From the beginning of the movement there was a strong tendency by its leaders to regard vocational education as so essentially different from other forms of education as to require separate planning, administrative and operating arrangements in almost every respect. In the opinion of many of its founders, the goals of vocational education were not the same as those of general education, and any attempt to combine the two was sure to result in failure. They believed that vocational education should be oriented entirely and exclusively toward immediate employment, and they saw little evidence that general studies contributed to vocational achievement.[2]

Starting from this premise, writers such as Wright and Allen developed a rationale which dealt with vocational education as being totally different. This led, among other things, to the position that no one without substantial experience in vocational education was qualified for a leadership role in it—a requirement which most of the early leaders themselves were at the outset unable to meet because of the recency of the movement. Nearly all of its early leaders came from the ranks of the general educators.

It is true that a number of general educators had opposed the introduction of vocational education into the schools. Some, like John Dewey, questioned it on philosophical grounds. Others believed that the training of workers for specific jobs was the responsibility of employers. Vocational advocates felt that the real reason for much of the opposition was prejudice against the manual worker by the educated group, and an attitude that practical education was unworthy of an equal place in the curriculum with the learned subjects. Wright and Allen, in another book, speak of administrators whose decisions have interfered with the efficiency of vocational education because their experience has been limited to the general education field.[3]

The authors of the Smith-Hughes law feared that unless specifically forbidden to do so the program might take certain directions which they believed to be unsound. To guard against this they wrote careful controls into the law. They did not want the funds to be spent for training in the professional occupations, as the land grant colleges had done. Therefore the law required that all instructions be of less than college grade, and not until this was changed by the Vocational Education Act of 1963 were funds available for programs beyond the secondary school. Secondly, they wanted the instruction to be of sufficient depth and thoroughness to assure the development of well trained, employable skilled workers. To provide this the law prescribed minimum allocations of instructional time for the teaching of practical and useful work skills. Third, they wished to minimize what they considered to be the negative and unsympathetic control of general educators over the program. This was done by placing the federal administration of vocational education under a newly created Federal Board for Vocational Education, with its own administrative staff, rather than to entrust it to the United States Office of Education which was responsible for federal relationships with general education in the nation.[4] States were required to establish State Boards of Vocational Education and employ specialized administrative personnel in order to share in the federal funds. However, the states were permitted to name the State Boards of Education which governed all other education to serve also as the State Board of Vocational Education, although some states did set up separate state governing boards to be responsible for vocational schools and programs. In 1946 the functions of the Federal Board for Vocational Education were absorbed by the United States Office of Education.

Commenting upon the reasons for separatist policies in the development of vocational education, David Snedden, an early spokesman, said that its early proponents believed that the regular school authorities were hostile to vocational education and to manual work and workers.[5]

Snedden and others believed that successful vocational education required close working relationships with occupational leaders, as indeed it does, but they felt that educators schooled in the tradition of general education were suspicious of employers and other industrial and business leaders, and did not relate well to them. They saw this aloofness and lack of rapport as another reason why vocational education should not be left in the hands of general educators.

This mistrust of the academic, the liberal and the general forms of education can be somewhat understood as a reaction to the unsympathetic and even hostile attitudes of some general educators toward the aims of vocational education and their unwillingness to accept it into the educational mainstream. Unfortunately, this has led to a spirit of competition which often finds the general educator and the vocational educator trying to claim the same student. In so reacting, perhaps over-reacting, vocational educators have continued, throughout the years, to question the value of much of the general education offered in the schools and to assert that most students would benefit more by vocational education. They have often attributed the predominance of general education to a desire by students and parents for academic respectability rather than to the value of general education itself. That this feeling still prevails among vocational educators is evident from a review of the program of the 1969 annual convention of the American Vocational Association. One of the major sections of this program was devoted to the theme "Incompatability—Human Needs and Academia." Two of the topics presented were entitled "The Grand Myth of Academic Respectability," and "The Impossible Dream—A Fantastic Failure." In this case the Impossible Dream is an academic education for all youth. It is the view of some influential vocational leaders that general academic education fails to meet the needs of many, perhaps most, American youth, and that it retains its place in the curriculum through a misplaced emphasis on prestige. They argue that vocational education should replace many of the academic studies now offered in the schools. A good many general critics of education also question the relevance and value of contemporary school curriculums, but they do not consider present forms of vocational education to be any better suited to the needs of youth for living in the modern world.

Levels and Degrees of Separatism

Separatism can manifest itself at three levels—the federal, the state and the local. At the federal level the 1917 legislation established complete administrative separation of vocational and general education through the creation of the Federal Board for Vocational Education. The separation of the policy making function at the state level was less complete, since the State Board of Education was permitted to act also as the State Board for Vocational Education. At the local level, vocational education, except in one or two states, became the responsibility of the local Board of Education which governed all elementary and secondary education in the district. This placed vocational programs under the administration of the local superintendent of schools, along with the program of general education. School superintendents usually come from the ranks of the general educators, and vocational educators have often expressed concern that such administrators may be biased against vocational education or too unfamiliar with it to recognize and respond to its special needs. For this reason they often recommend that each local school system appoint an administrator for the vocational program who is experienced in the field of vocational education and who reports directly to the superintendent of schools rather than to one of his subordinates.

The feeling of need for separate status is what gives rise to the continuing effort of vocational education leaders to maintain a position of power and accessibility as close as possible to the top of the educational hierarchy in all public education agencies. If complete separation of the control of vocational education from general education is not desirable or practical (and many vocational educators concede that it is neither), then the fears which create the demand for separatism can be diminished by assuring vocational education of equal attention and support with general education in educational policy making. This is the real meaning of the sensitivity shown by vocational leaders to the rank and status of vocational adminstrators at federal, state and local levels relative to administrators of general education.

The American Vocational Association has often deplored what it considers to be the downgrading of the status of vocational education in the United States Office of Education because the rank assigned to the top vocational administrator in that office is lower than it was formerly. A newsletter supported by the American Vocational Association reiterates this criticism in an issue published in January, 1970.[6] Despite the great increase in support for vocational education, financially and otherwise, which has been demonstrated by Congress since 1963, many vocational educators remain unhappy because it does not play a stronger role on the educational scene.

Some of the early leaders of vocational education likened the program to the infant industries which struggled to establish themselves in America after the nation was founded, in competition with European manufacturers. These industries were given protection through tariffs so that they could have a chance to develop and those directing vocational education at its beginning felt that it too needed protection, even from some of its avowed friends, if it was to have a fair start.[7] Their hope was that this would take the form of separate administration and control in order to prevent the general educators from weakening or emasculating the program. Yet they realized that the possibility of a completely separate system was remote and they accepted the concept of unitary control in the states and local communities.[8]

These views are significant because they express the concerns of vocational educators during the formative years of the movement and because these concerns have by no means vanished from the thinking of present-day vocational leaders. They help us to understand why the question of separatism between vocational and general education continues to be an issue in American education.

Justification For Separatism

Vocational policy makers have suggested a number of reasons why they believe that vocational education requires a large degree of autonomy and administrative independence from general education. Among them are the following.

The goals of vocational education and general, academic education are quite different.

General educators are too often unsympathetic to the work oriented goals of vocational education and vocational students. They do not understand or value the world of work because they have never been a part of it. They do not relate well to persons in business, industry, trade or commerce because these activities are outside the field of their own experience. Therefore, if they control or administer vocational education they will at best accept it grudgingly and at worst 'deny it the means for success.

The vocational curriculum, as seen by the vocational specialists, should consist exclusively of the skills and technical knowledge of a particular occupation. General education is largely irrelevant in such a curriculum, except for some aspects of mathematics and science as they apply directly to an occupation. Therefore it is better not to mix general education with vocational education.

The primary qualification of a vocational teacher is occupational competence, not academic credentials, and the best measure of occupational competence is length and breadth of occupational experience. Those with academic backgrounds often fail to appreciate this and vocational teachers are not given proper recognition or support by those who do not understand their program.

Vocational education, to be efficient, calls for large blocks of the students' time if the necessary work skills are to be developed. The daily time schedules of academic programs are often in conflict with this need, so it is better to keep the two programs separate.

Vocational education requires that enough students pursuing

the same occupation be brought together to permit group instruction with a reasonable degree of economy. This can usually be done only by combining in a separate school students from several other schools who wish to train for the same occupation.

Good vocational instruction demands that the student be trained in facilities which resemble as closely as possible those of actual employment, using the same type of equipment found on the job. This often means very specialized facilities and specialized, expensive equipment, both of which can best be provided in a separate school devoted entirely to the task of occupational preparation.

A school having no other purpose than vocational training can concentrate on this objective and will be more efficient because its resources and efforts will not be dissipated by general education demands.

The Validity of Justifications For Separatism

Since vocational education was introduced into the schools there have been those who questioned the validity of some of these assumptions. They have felt, and many continue to feel, that in educational terms more is lost than gained by organizing vocational education as a separate discipline, particularly in the high school.

It is interesting to note that two large areas of vocational education have never been separated from the general high school and its program. These are business education, including the distributive occupations, and agricultural education. From the beginning these have been incorporated as additional subjects in existing high schools, to be pursued as major or elective subjects by students whose needs and interests they could serve. Nor has occupational experience in depth been placed ahead of academic credentials for teachers of these subjects. Yet, as measured by job placements of graduates and their success on the job, both agricultural and business education have been more effective than most of the other fields in which vocational education has engaged, and together they have enrolled the largest numbers.

Not everyone agrees that the goals of vocational and general education are so different as to require a completely different educational context. Most people recognize that when a reasonably stable career choice has been made, and if it requires extended specialized preparation, those who have chosen it must separate from those with other career goals in order to pursue their own. However, there is increasing evidence that the high school years are too early for most young people to make serious and lasting career decisions and to act upon them by entering into a formal training program. Studies by Ginzberg, Super, and Flanagan, among others, show that career choices made before the age of high school graduation are tentative and unstable and strongly suggest that preparation for a particular occupation be delayed until then.[9, 10] Brookover and Nosow, as a result of a sociological study of vocational education questioned the early commitment to a specific occupation.[11] The whole issue of the relationship between general and vocational education is considered at greater length in a subsequent chapter, and, as we shall see once again, is much influenced by the perceptions held by different individuals of the goals of occupational education.

That vocational education is any longer handicapped by the antagonism of academic educators, or their lack of support when it is placed under their control, seems most unlikely. No research has ever been done to verify this fear or to determine whether alleged unfavorable attitudes on the part of general administrators have undergone changes over the years. An extensive study of the attitudes of school board members in New York state toward occupational education was completed in 1969. It showed that the majority of these officials, who control educational policy in their communities, have strong positive attitudes toward vocational education.[12] Although the study did not test the attitudes of administrators, these board members are the ones who select and employ the superintendents of schools, and it is unlikely that they would tend to choose administrators who would be opposed to the policies they favor.

The Panel of Consultants on Vocational Education of 1961 and The National Advisory Council on Vocational Education of 1967 were both headed by well-known general educators, the first by Dr. Benjamin C. Willis, Superintendent of Schools of Chicago, Illinois, and the second by Dr. Martin Essex, Superintendent of Public Education for the State of Ohio. Both groups produced positive, constructive reports, strongly urging more and better vocational education. Each report resulted in landmark federal legislation providing wider goals and greatly increased resources for vocational education. James B. Conant, a general educator whose views have helped to shape public education to a greater extent than almost any other individual during the 1960s, has given warm support to vocational education. Such actions are not consistent with the charges still made by vocationalists that vocational education is held back and denied its rightful place by the negative attitudes of general educators. In actual fact, occupational education today is organized and administered as a part of the public school system of the nation and as such it is subject to the leadership of general educators and administrators at federal, state and local levels. There is no real evidence that vocational education suffers from this arrangement.

The belief that vocational education demands larger blocks of instructional time than the general school program can accommodate is not borne out by the experience of business education or agricultural education. Both of these programs have succeeded within the scheduling framework of the general or comprehensive school. With the growing trend toward modular and flexible scheduling in the schools there seems to be no reason why occupational education must seek a separate school organization to achieve its purposes. At least during the high school years, having students devote as much as half their learning time to vocational training, as earlier programs required, cannot be justified, because it leaves too little time for essential general studies. It is significant that the Vocational Education Act of 1963 eliminated this requirement.

The need to bring together enough students in the same occupation to permit economical group instruction rests upon the assumption that the instruction is to be so occupationally specific that it has nothing in common with any other occupation. Many vocationalists believe this should be the case, but there is much reason to question it, and it is increasingly difficult to defend at the high school level. Similar questions can be raised regarding highly specialized facilities and equipment, except for post high school programs.

The greater effectiveness of the separate school in producing a better trained vocational graduate has not been demonstrated. As we examine the question of the merits of the comprehensive and the separate school, more evidence of this will be cited.

The Separate and the Comprehensive School

The tendency toward separation on the part of vocational education expresses itself sharply in discussions concerning the separate vs the comprehensive school. Many of the early leaders felt that successful vocational education could take place only in separate vocational schools. On the other hand, other educators hold strong views to the contrary, and they believe there are decided advantages to having vocational education become a part of the regular school program. In 1918 the Commission on the Reorganization of Secondary Education of the NEA submitted a report which set forth seven cardinal objectives or principles for the secondary school curriculum. Among them were the vocational objectives, and the Commission recommended that general and vocational education should be carried on side by side in the secondary schools. A number of vocational educators, among them Snedden, at once took issue with this suggestion.[13] Snedden's concept of the nature and range of the vocational curriculum, which will be discussed in Chapter 4, caused him to reject the plan for comprehensive high schools as unrealistic and ineffective, and the majority of vocational educators, other than those in business and agriculture, have continued to advocate the separate school for conducting their programs. The proliferation of the separate area vocational school since its recognition by the Vocational Education Act of 1963 attests to its popularity among them.

The comprehensive high school is presumed to meet the needs of all the youth of a community by including curriculums for the college bound, for those with specialized interests and talents such as music and art, and also for those who desire occupational preparation. Vocational leaders usually contend that such a school cannot perform this task adequately because it cannot offer training in a sufficient number of occupations to be truly comprehensive. They maintain that this can only be done by establishing separate vocational schools. This, of course, raises the question as to how many occupations must be included in a school's curricular offerings to make it comprehensive, and on this there is no agreement. Conant, who supports the comprehensive school, has suggested that a high school should offer courses in five occupations in addition to its business courses. Yet when separate vocational schools are established they seldom offer many more. If it was possible to follow the work history of all of the graduates of a large high school who do not enroll for further education, the number of occupations in which they would later be found would be so numerous and so diverse that no school, comprehensive or separate, could possibly provide training for all of them. Therefore, in terms of the future occupational needs of all of its students, the number of occupations for which any school can prepare students must be very limited. The Vocational Education Act of 1963 authorizes support for area vocational schools having as few as five occupational curriculums. An area school, set up as a separate school, seldom has more than a dozen occupations represented in its curriculum offerings, and these are likely to be predominantly in the skilled craft and industrial occupations. Thus, if the comprehensive high school cannot satisfy the requirement of comprehensiveness because its occupational offerings are too limited, the separate vocational school cannot claim to do much better.

As to whether the separate school is more effective than the comprehensive school in preparing for occupational life, until recently there was little except opinion upon which to base a conclusion. Since 1960, however, some significant research has been done on this subject. A national study by Eninger compared the placements of some five thousand graduates of separate and comprehensive high schools in the occupations for which they were trained.[14] Placements from neither type of school were impressive, averaging about thirty percent of those graduated. There was a very slight advantage to the graduate of the separate school, but the difference was too small to establish any real superiority in this respect. It was attributed to the fact that the separate school more often had a staff member with special responsibility for the placement of graduates, and it is reasonable to assume that if the comprehensive school were to add this service this difference between the two schools would disappear. Another study, by Kaufman and Schaefer, conducted in the northeastern United States, found no difference in placement records, employer satisfaction or success on the job between graduates from separate and comprehensive schools.[15]

Whether occupational education can be as effective in a comprehensive school as in a separate school, with an identity of its own, is already becoming a policy issue in the development of the rapidly growing two-year colleges and area vocational schools across the country. Wherever they are permitted to do so vocational educators are planning separate vocational schools, often on a regional basis, serving the needs of several adjacent school districts. New York and Ohio, among other states, are moving in this direction. On the other hand, a number of the largest cities which have long maintained separate vocational schools are turning away from them to the comprehensive high school.[16] The two-year college is the fastest growing educational institution in the nation at the present time. It is also the type of school where occupational education is experiencing its greatest growth.[17] Its most common form is the community college, in which liberal arts and occupational preparatory programs are offered under the same roof. Both programs can be terminal or they can lead to transfer by the student to a four-year institution for further study. The forerunners of some of these schools were the earlier mechanics institutes or technical institutes, which were separate vocational schools, terminal in character, having no liberal arts offerings. To meet modern demands they have, in many cases, had to become comprehensive, and as new two-year colleges are created, they also tend to be comprehensive. Those responsible for the occupational curriculums in the two-year colleges often complain that their programs receive too little attention and support from the administrative officers who head their schools and that the liberal arts areas are more favored by students and administration. They feel that the career oriented programs would be more effective if offered in a separate institution, but this would seem to be an unnecessary and costly way to meet the problem. There are certain circumstances, however, which could cause public policy to turn to the separate post secondary vocational school, and these will be discussed in Chapter 6.

In general, educational and social thinking is increasingly opposed to the whole concept of separating vocational and general education. Just as educational separatism on racial grounds has become unacceptable to most Americans, so any form of educational apartheid based on the occupational future of young people is being rejected. It leads to undesirable status distinctions between individuals because of their occupational choices and to false superiority-inferiority attitudes toward equally essential aspects of education. The American Vocational Association, in announcing its work program for 1970-1975 devotes a section to the need for unifying general and vocational education and states that a major goal of the American Vocational Association and its membership will be that of working with general educators to assist in improving education at all levels (K—to the grave).[18] The report of the 1967 Advisory Council on Vocational Education concludes that vocational education is not a separate discipline within education, but is a basic objective of all education and must be a basic element of each person's education. And Venn, in his excellent study of vocational education expresses the current viewpoint very well when he says that the separate but equal approach to vocational and technical education is unsound.[19]

Other Educational Losses Through Separatism

There are other losses. Long ago it was pointed out that if two forms of separately administered education are competing for public funds, taxpayers and the public are confused and distracted by the rival claims for recognition and support.[20] Competition for the tax dollar tends to weaken the extent to which education can present a united front on behalf of support for education as a whole. The separate approach to educational services also results in a competition for students and a never ending controversy as to how many and what kind of students should pursue general rather than occupationally specialized goals. The greater the amount of separatism the more the vocational student becomes identified as a terminal student, with less educational potential than other students and with lower aspirations. Although this may be far from the truth, it causes many able students and many parents to avoid courses and programs of an occupational nature because of the image of vocational education as being inferior.[21] The whole question of comparative status and prestige is sharpened and made more difficult to reconcile when the two aspects of education are separated instead of combined.

There are losses also to the professional workers in both general and vocational education. The vocational educator feels only a partial identification with the education profession as a whole. He has his own professional organizations, often not affiliated with those of general education, and only infrequently does he become active in professional activities which relate to education at large. The same tends to be true of the general educator with respect to vocational education, so that both groups lose the opportunity for understanding the problems of the other and of enjoying the wider educational horizons which come from sharing the common problems of American education. The more complete the separation the more isolated the vocational educator tends to become from the broader educational scene.[22]

Summary

The spirit of separation between general and vocational education in American schools began early in the history of the vocational movement. It sprang primarily from two sources. One was the belief of vocational leaders that learning an occupation was so essentially different from learning the disciplines of general education as to require an entirely different approach—one which was not compatible with usual school policies and practices. The other was the conviction that if the control and administration of vocational education were assigned to persons having only general education experience they would, through lack of understanding or, in some cases, their hostility toward practical training, defeat the purposes of vocational education and cause it to fail. On the other hand, general educators have at times displayed negative attitudes toward vocational education and vocational educators. This lack of mutual trust and acceptance on the part of both groups has not yet completely disappeared. At times some vocational leaders still disparage general education, and characterize it as more or less ornamental and useless, designed for an elite minority, but still dominating the school curriculum through the false prestige of academic respectability.

Public policy, nevertheless, has not permitted vocational education a completely separate role, and it has had to function, for the most part, within the same framework as general education. Despite the fears and misgivings of some vocationalists there is no real evidence that it has been damaged by this arrangement. Within the limitations which this imposes vocational leaders have tried to maintain a separate identity for the program, and in whatever ways possible have favored separatism. Their strong preference for the separate vocational school rather than the comprehensive school is but one illustration of this. At the present time, wherever state policies will permit, separate area vocational schools are being established. In curriculum development, teacher education, and leadership training the differences with general education are still accentuated.

There is growing realization that it is no longer possible to compartmentalize education into general, academic and vocational components and that to continue any form of separatism in education is self-defeating. Technology has brought us to the point where the success factors of most occupations cannot be identified as the separate products of either vocational or general education. This makes it both futile and wasteful to continue to foster an increasingly artificial distinction between the two.

Whatever the reasons may be for the separatism of vocational education, American education and American society pay a price for it. It prevents vocational education from contributing fully to the needs of the society, and it deprives education of the full benefits of what ought to be one of its greatest resources.

REFERENCES

1. Wright, John C., and Allen, Charles R. *The Supervision of Vocational Education.* New York: John Wiley and Sons, 1926.
2. Snedden, David. *Vocational Education.* New York: Macmillan Co., 1920.
3. Wright, John C., and Allen, Charles R. *The Administration of Vocational Education.* New York: John Wiley and Sons, 1926.
4. U. S. Congress. *Smith-Hughes Act.* Public Law 347, 64th Cong., 1917.
5. Snedden. *Vocational Education.*
6. *Vocational Education and Manpower Reporter* 2, no. 1 (January, 1970).
7. Snedden. *Vocational Education.*
8. Ibid.
9. Super, Donald. *Vocational Guidance and Career Development: Selected Readings,* compiled by H. J. Peters and J. C. Hansen. New York: Macmillan Co., 1966.
10. Ginzberg, Eli. *Vocational Education,* edited by M. Barlow. National Association for the Study of Education, Sixty-Fourth Yearbook. Chicago: University of Chicago Press, 1965.
11. Brookover, William B., and Nosow, Sigmund. "A Sociological Analysis of Vocational Education in the United States." *Education for a Changing World of Work.* Report of the Panel of Consultants on Vocational Education, Appendix III, 00E-80021. Washington, D. C.: U. S. Government Printing Office, 1963.

12. Western New York State Education Department, Division of Research. *Attitudes of School Board Members Toward Occupational Education.* Albany, N. Y.: Division of Research, State Education Dept., 1969.

13. Snedden. *Vocational Education.*

14. Eninger, Max. *The Process and Products of T and I High School Level Vocational Education in the United States.* Pittsburgh: American Institute for Research, 1965.

15. Kaufman, Jacob, and Schaefer, Carl. *The Role of the Secondary School in Preparing Youth for Employment.* Pennsylvania State University, 1967.

16. New York City Board of Education. *Policy Decisions on Comprehensive High Schools.* Brooklyn: New York City Board of Education (November, 1967).

17. Advisory Council on Vocational Education. *Vocational Education: The Bridge Between Man and His Work.* Washington, D. C.: U. S. Department of Health, Education and Welfare, Office of Education, 1968.

18. "Program of Work: 1970-1975: AVA in Action." *American Vocational Journal* 45, no. 2 (February, 1970): 88.

19. Venn, Grant. *Man, Education and Work.* Washington, D. C.: The American Council on Education, 1964.

20. Snedden. *Vocational Education.*

21. DeCarlo, Charles. *New Conceptions of Vocational and Technical Education,* edited by J. Rosenberg. New York: Teachers College Press, 1967.

22. Leighbody, Gerald. "Impact of the Area Vocational School." *Educational Leadership.* Washington, D. C.: Association for Supervision and Curriculum Development (April, 1968).

CHAPTER 3

CHOOSING AND LEARNING
AN OCCUPATION

Occupational education cannot continue to concern itself solely with those who have made a career choice and wish to prepare for it. It must also take a major responsibility for assisting in the process of making that choice.

Career orientation and planning are a part of vocational education, although at present they are treated as something which precedes it. Vocational educators have usually felt that their task begins only after career planning has been completed and a vocational choice has been made. They have long been dissatisfied because career orientation in the schools has been ineffective or completely lacking, but on the whole they have considered this to be the responsibility of others. They have expected that vocational orientation and guidance would bring them students who are interested in the occupations they are prepared to teach, and well qualified to succeed in them. That is, they have viewed career planning as a recruiting and selection device for vocational students, but have assumed that it is to be carried on by guidance counselors and other school personnel. They have nearly always been disappointed in the results because they have failed to recognize that choosing an occupation and learning an occupation are inseparable parts of the same process. There is a continuum here that does not permit separation into discrete stages. Vocational educators cannot expect that guidance counselors, parents and others will be responsible for career orientation, while they themselves stand aside and wait for well informed and counseled students to arrive on their doorstep ready to be trained.[1]

All of the federal vocational education legislation since 1946 has provided funds and authority for vocational educators to enter actively into the area of vocational and career guidance. Yet very little has been done about it, although there is no form of education which has a greater stake in helping future workers to choose wisely before they undertake serious preparation for reaching their occupational goals. Congressman Roman Pucinski of Illinois has devoted much time to the study of vocational education and is one of its staunchest supporters, but in a recent speech he urged that career development, rather than mere job training, become the primary goal of vocational educational.

Learning About the World of Work

Choosing an occupation which will lead to a satisfying and productive vocational life has become progressively more difficult for youth in our society. The vast number of possible career choices which are available in our increasingly complex economy poses a problem at the outset. The well defined occupations have been studied and classified in the *Dictionary of Occupational Titles,* published by the United States Department of Labor, and this is periodically revised and updated. Each new edition shows a significant increase in the number and variety of jobs and the most recent edition lists more than 25,000. It is no longer easy to sample a variety of occupations before deciding upon a career direction. Unless a young person follows the occupation of the father or mother, few parents, even among the well educated, can be of much assistance to their children as career counselors. They feel as uninformed and confused as the youth they would like to help.

Choosing an occupation is more than just selecting a means for earning an income. It is also a choice of social status, personal associates, tastes, preferences and life style of the individual. Not only his talents but also his temperament and his value system are involved in the choice. On the other hand, practical considerations require that the social and economic need for workers in various occupations and the short term and long term prospects of those needs also be taken into account.

It is increasingly difficult for children and youth to become acquainted with the world of work through direct experience or through first hand observation of adults at work. Except for public contact jobs, more and more work is carried on in specialized settings which young people in their daily living have no opportunity to observe. The age at which young people can expect to be first employed continues to rise, reducing the chance to learn through holding juvenile jobs. In simpler societies, and in the earlier days of our own society, work was a part of daily family life, entered into and observed by children from their early years, and the skills required were often taught by parents. There was no problem of work orientation. Work in our own highly technological society is totally different, and the transition from youth to adult life and to work is much more difficult. For a young person to enter into any specialized program of training for a particular occupation with inadequate knowledge of its nature or of its suitability for him is a waste of human resources and is educationally and economically unsound. This is why it is essential that an informed and intelligent choice be arrived at before any person, young or older, enters into a serious program of occupational training.

With increasing frequency those who are aware of this are urging that vocational education begin as a program of orientation to the world of work, that it start in the early grades of school, continue through the secondary period, and culminate with specialized preparation in grades thirteen and fourteen. Clearly, those who recommend this do not advocate any form of job skill training in the elementary or middle grades, and only generalized skills in the high school. They distinguish between learning about occupations and learning an occupation, and they include both in their new definition of vocational education. This view is not readily accepted by many vocationalists, who continue to see their task almost entirely in terms of specific occupational preparation. Yet there is growing evidence that certain facts, concepts, social skills and attitudes are common success factors in all occupations and should be taught to students at all educational levels. This is stressed in the report of the Summer Study on Occupational, Vocational and Technical Education sponsored by the Massachusetts Institute of Technology in 1965.[2] It is emphasized in the writings of Marvin Feldman, Vocational Specialist of the Staff of the Ford Foundation, and by other specialists in vocational education.[3, 4, 5]

Teaching About the World of Work

Despite the growing recognition of the need for occupational orientation as a part of every student's education there has been little effort made to meet it. Curriculum specialists, vocational experts and teachers will ultimately have to take the responsibility for its development. Whenever an emerging social need becomes so important that it must be accorded a place in the school curriculum it tends to be treated as a new subject or discipline which must be somehow inserted into an already crowded list of learnings. What little has been done to teach about the world of work has usually been approached in this way. It has frequently taken the form of a course of study, often labeled as the Study of Occupations, and too often taught by a teacher having minimum knowledge, training or enthusiasm for the task. Much of the time in such courses is spent in cataloging major occupational areas and listing certain standard types of information relating to them. Such courses are invariably dull, pedantic and theoretical, providing little insight and less stimulation, and few of them survive very long. However the need for occupational orientation is to be met, this is clearly not the way to do it.

In our society the ultimate choice of a vocation comes at the end of a long and developmental process.[6] We like to believe that it is a totally free choice on the part of every individual, and in the sense that no one is assigned to any particular occupation this is true. Yet those whose choice is limited by lack of knowledge about the choices available have this freedom seriously reduced. It is also true that committing one's self to an occupation at too early an age effectively limits the range of choice by precluding the consideration of others.[7]

The question of how to include the needed knowledge and skill of career planning as essential learnings in the education of all youth is not easy to answer. We have already observed that simple data gathering and fact stuffing are inadequate and ineffective, as is any attempt to consider it as another discipline to be added to the list of required school subjects. The idea of exploring occupations through a series of work sampling experiences has often been suggested and occasionally tried. The industrial arts program in the schools can furnish exploratory experiences for certain occupations, but they do not go much beyond those in industrial manufacturing. In an economy where only about one third of the jobs are of this type, students are still left without exposure to the majority of careers which they might consider. One of the best means for learning about an occupation is to work at it, and the work experience or cooperative work-study form of education has proved to be very valuable for this purpose. It often helps a student to learn that certain types of occupations are not attractive to him or that he is ill suited for them, and this is surely useful career knowledge. Yet the work-study program cannot be made available until the latter years of high school because of age restrictions on the employment of young people in most states. Field trips to observe and study the nature and environment of various types of occupations have been used with some success, but generally speaking no systematic or sustained attempts have been made to provide the learning experiences which are required, and additional, new approaches are badly needed.

Vocational educators have been reluctant to use their time or teaching facilities to help youth explore occupations which they may decide not to pursue, because they have felt that they should concentrate on training the student who has already selected an occupation. They have looked upon career planning and choice as an important adjunct to vocational education but not an integral part of it, and they have based their instruction on the assumption that they are the job trainers while guidance counselors are the career advisors. This must change. Vocational leaders and teachers will have to become directly involved in forms of career planning and vocational decision making which will begin at least as early as the intermediate grades of the elementary school. For those who are convinced of this it is very encouraging that the American Vocational Association in its program of work approved at the Dallas convention in 1968 has set forth as one of its goals that vocational educators must become involved in the promotion and implementation of programs of occupational orientation.

The Process of Career Choice

We have much to learn about the whole process by which people in present-day America arrive at the careers which they finally pursue. There has been enough research, however, to establish some basis for assisting young persons in this increasingly difficult aspect of their lives. Among the things that seem fairly clear are these:

Career decision making is very much an individual experience. It is influenced by many things which happen or fail to happen to the individual during childhood and youth.

Vocational choice does not occur at a particular point in time but is a culmination of many experiences and influences in the daily life of growing youth. It is closely related to the value system which the individual forms as a result of these influences.

The age at which a vocational decision becomes reasonably stable varies rather widely with individuals, but several studies suggest that it seldom occurs before the age of eighteen. In many cases it may be later. This is why Ginzberg, a long time researcher in this field, recommends that specialized vocational training be deferred until after the high school period.[8]

Career choice is partly a product of cultural conditioning and societal norms and the technologically dominated American culture of the late twentieth century has brought about certain social and economic influences which tend to prolong the period of career decision making. For one thing, the rising sophistication of most kinds of work requires longer periods of basic and general education, as well as more and longer specialized training. Much of this training can be secured only on the job but this conflicts with another result of modern technology—the fact that fewer workers are required for the same output of goods and services. This reduction in required manpower is achieved partly at the expense of the younger, beginning worker. Legislation which has continually increased the legal minimum wage also tends to reduce the teenager's chances for employment, because his output often does not warrant the artificially high wages which are mandated. At the same time the overall wealth of the nation is increasingly capable of supporting youth in school for longer periods. These and other factors combine to slowly raise the age of entry into full-time employment, and one effect of this is to lengthen the period which most young people can have to decide upon career goals. What we have not recognized is that this extended time is of little value unless well planned programs of career orientation are provided. Without them our young people experience only a longer period of floundering and uncertainty regarding career plans, and this can only lead to social unrest and strain.

Counseling and Admitting Students Into Vocational Courses

In the absence of any really effective occupational planning many young people who enroll in vocational courses at the present time do so for the wrong reasons. At the same time, many students who could benefit from occupational education are not served by it because of its limited objectives.[9] Some elect vocational courses because a choice is forced upon them at the time they enter high school, or soon thereafter, between a so-called college entrance curriculum and a vocational curriculum. Neither they nor their parents are prepared to make such a choice, which all too often is irrevocable, and it should not be required of them. Others have formed a dislike for school and the studies it requires and mistakenly believe that they will escape from further academic demands by choosing a vocational program. Probably the most common reason why a student enters a vocational course is the judgment of teachers and counselors that he is not "college material," and those who make such decisions usually have in mind a four-year liberal arts or professional preparatory institution. This gives rise to the familiar college-non-college syndrome that is accepted by so many educators, on the theory that those who should attend college can be identified early from those who should not and that the non-college group should then follow a vocational program. In reality there is no valid way to make such a distinction, or to determine in advance who should terminate his education at what point. At the present time more than forty percent of those who complete high school continue into further education and this proportion is increasing rapidly with the spreading availability of the two-year college. This is why the report of the Summer Study of the Massachusetts Institute of Technology recommended that, "High school education should not be considered terminal for any student. The education of all senior high school students should be directed toward continued education; in apprenticeship, in pre-job and on the job education, in post high school occupationally oriented institutions, or in liberal arts colleges, professional colleges, or two year baccalaureate transfer programs of junior colleges."[10]

Being convinced that the success of vocational education can be measured only by job placement and subsequent job success, vocational educators have usually felt that they need to ascertain in advance the success potential of students who are admitted to vocational courses. In the absence of valid devices for predicting such success they have turned to more generalized measures which may be even less valid, or perhaps irrelevant. Among the qualities which are often sought in prospective vocational students are satisfactory school grades, good school attendance, evidence of developed work disciplines, general intelligence, absence of previous disciplinary problems, and strong motivation toward learning. Whenever vocational teachers are asked to list the characteristics of students who should be admitted to their courses, the description is almost always that of the idealized student. The student they would like to have is one who has already achieved the positive work habits and attitudes, the high motivation, and the general education skills which in fact should be the outcome rather than the prerequisites of good vocational instruction.

Vocational teachers frequently complain that they are required to accept mostly the "poor" student. They may not realize that the "better" student they desire has the ability to learn readily almost any occupation in which he becomes interested and that he already possesses most of the generalized skills necessary for vocational success. On the other hand it is precisely the poor student, not favored by vocational educators, who most needs to develop the general skills and work attitudes which vocational education is so well suited to provide. These include planning the work task, organizing to accomplish it, following systematic procedures, checking for progress, persisting to completion and accepting responsibility for the outcome. The student who is disadvantaged socially, economically, and culturally is not likely to have many of the qualities which vocational (and other) educators would like to see in their students. The vocational educator has been particularly reluctant to accept and serve the disadvantaged student, partly because he is anxious to improve the image of vocational education and to avoid the impression that it is designed for academic failures. These problems will be discussed more fully in later chapters, but it is clear that the mandates of the 1963 and 1968 Vocational Education Acts to meet the needs of the disadvantaged can no longer be neglected or ignored.

In the future the admission of students into vocational courses will need to involve a longer and much improved program of career guidance and planning; it will also need to include more tryout and experimentation, through work experience and other means, and the opportunity to change early career plans readily without educational penalties.

The Prediction of Occupational Success

It is understandable that counselors, manpower specialists, and vocational educators would like to have some means for determining the potential of an individual for success in an occupation before investing time and money in preparing him for it. It is as much to the advantage of the individual as to society to know in advance, if possible, which occupation is best suited for him, and especially so if lengthy specialized training is involved. Unfortunately, the early prediction of future success of individuals in any human endeavor is extremely difficult. The process is especially fraught with danger when such predictions are attempted at too early an age and when the results of the predictions substantially reduce the range of other career choices.

Ideally, such devices should have good predictive reliability and should be capable of being administered easily and quickly. Needless to say, a great deal of effort has been invested in attempts to develop such instruments. They usually take the form of pencil and paper tests, indexes and inventories, supplemented by interviews. Up to this time, however, the results have been quite discouraging when subjected to any rigorous evaluation. Among the factors which may account for this is the extreme complexity of the psycho-socio patterns which determine for the individual his job success and job satisfaction potential. Another is the great and growing number and diversity of occupational categories in a modern technological society.

John O. Crites, Director of the University Counseling Service of the University of Iowa has analyzed the capacity of existing instruments to predict what he considers to be the two essential elements of vocational adjustment. These are:

> How well the individual performs his job
> How much job satisfaction he enjoys.

His analysis leads him to conclude that most of our assessment instruments have little or no predictive value in forecasting these two major criteria of vocational adjustment.[11] He further points out that the correlations between intelligence and job success are low to moderate and that there is no correlation between vocational interest inventory scores and job satisfaction. These are very significant findings and they must raise serious questions about the value of some of the most widely used tools in present-day counseling.

A great deal of vocational counseling and advisement in the past has been based upon the so-called trait-factor theory. This theory assumes that different occupations require different functional attributes on the part of the worker and that these can be identified and then matched by traits which can in turn be identified in individuals. This would make possible the matching, in advance, of people to jobs, and would at least avoid the "square peg in the round hole" problem in relation to occupational choice. Many past and present attempts to predict occupational success rest on this concept. Crites questions the wisdom of this approach. He believes it is too simplistic because it overlooks the complex and developmental nature of choosing, entering and succeeding in an occupation.[12]

Rather than being best suited for a particular occupation, it is more likely that most persons can succeed in any one of a wide variety of occupations, none of which are necessarily related. The one which is ultimately followed depends upon familiarity, opportunity and interest, and these in turn depend upon sociological and economic environment, largely fortuitous.

Probably the most extensive and sustained research on the subject of predicting occupational success has been conducted by the Employment Security Branch of the United States Department of Labor. Beginning in 1935 a testing device known as the General Aptitude Test Battery (GATB) has been under development and refinement, for use by job counselors of this agency. The theoretical framework for this battery rests upon the assumption that an inexperienced, untrained individual having a test profile similar to a successful experienced worker will be likely to become equally successful in the same kind of occupation. Job success is determined chiefly by the judgment of the supervisor of the experienced worker. There are important weaknesses in the conceptual framework of this approach, but even if these are overlooked, an examination of the correlations between GATB scores and measures of job success reveals that few are high, many are low, and the rest are moderate. Additionally, many of the correlations result from a very small number of cases.[3] For this reason the test results are interpreted by agency counselors with considerable caution, and the only recommendations made are those of possible suitability for a broad category of occupations. No reliable norms have been established for persons under seventeen years of age, which should serve as a caution to those who would seek to predict the occupational future of adolescent youth.

Vocational teachers and leaders have generally accepted the theory of matching individuals with jobs and also the concept that the decision for a particular occupation is a single, point-in-time episode in the life of the individual. The organization and administration of past and present vocational programs reflect these beliefs. So does the design of the total school organization, because it forces students to make choices at specified and uniform grades and ages which either commit them to a specific occupation or foreclose their opportunities to pursue certain others. Vocational courses are planned on the assumption that those who enroll in them have made a clear-cut occupational choice, that it is stable, and that the student will follow the occupation he has prepared for when the training is complete. Program success is measured in these terms. Recent research shows that vocational students benefit little from their training unless these conditions are fully met.[14] If these requirements must be met it is easy to see why vocational educators are so preoccupied with finding means for predicting occupational success, so that students may be properly screened for admission to their courses. Unfortunately, the lack of any reliable method for making such predictions continues to defeat their efforts

As we gain more understanding of the dynamics of vocational choice, and perhaps become less convinced of the possibility of matching people with future jobs, objectives and patterns of occupational education will have to be considerably modified if they are to be compatible with the realities of occupational life. There is a good possibility that it may never be possible to invent instruments which can satisfactorily predict how well suited an individual may be for a particular occupation, because the conceptual basis for such instruments may be faulty. The idea that certain traits, aptitudes and potentials which match the requirements for some particular occupation are dormant in an individual and can be revealed by tests and interviews becomes increasingly doubtful with every additional research into the nature of career choice. This suggests that perhaps attempts to prepare adolescent youth for specific occupations should give way to efforts to achieve the following:

1. The development of those generalized skills, attitudes and powers which are applicable to and demanded by all occupations.
2. The opportunity to perform work samples of numerous types of occupations, under the guidance and observation of qualified teacher-counselors—not to prepare for a particular occupation—but to help decide which occupation to select and prepare for.
3. The opportunity for every adolescent to secure some actual work experience as a part of the whole process of career decision making.[15]

Occupational education could then culminate its service by providing specialized job preparation for these same young people as post-adolescents and adults who have made more sound and stable occupational choices.

Vocational Education and the Slow Learner

Teachers generally have tended to confuse a slower pace of learning with inability to learn. Schools are so organized that a measured amount of learning must be accomplished each year of the student's life, and those whose learning style and rate of progress fall short of this find little or no provision in the schools to accommodate them. They are labeled as slow learners and they become more overage, out of phase and misfit with each successive year in school. A student who is slower to achieve in school directed tasks is soon considered to have a lower learning potential than those who learn faster, although in reality there may be little relation between potential and pace. Such students may be able to reach much higher learning levels than either they or their teachers believe possible, if given time and encouragement. Unfortunately they seldom receive either.

Because the so-called slow learner appears to many counselors and teachers to be incapable of succeeding in academic studies, he is often advised to enter a vocational curriculum. He may be quite willing to do so, in the mistaken belief that he will escape the need to deal with the book oriented studies which he has come to dislike, and be able to spend his time in practical activities leading to some kind of occupation. This usually turns out not to be true. Most occupations today demand more technical knowledge and general knowledge than manual skills, and the student soon finds himself once again studying books and manuals and dealing with verbal concepts and academic learnings. At the same time, vocational educators often resent the idea that their program should be selected as suitable chiefly for the rejects from the academic courses. Once again the slow learner is likely to find himself unwanted, and in a program which is no better designed to meet his needs than the standard academic curriculum.

In many ways occupational education is better adapted to the needs of the slower learner than any other form of education, if the vocational educator will accept him. By its nature the instruction has to be largely individual, and group teaching and learning play a far less important role than they do in the more traditional subjects. This makes it possible, if properly planned, for each learner to proceed at his own pace, without much relation to the progress of others, and this is exactly what the slow learner must do. If the student has a genuine interest in pursuing the occupation he is learning, many of the other aspects of his education which otherwise lack meaning and reality for him can become significant. Thus, for him, vocational education becomes important as a learning process, as well as for its substance.

This does not mean that only the slow learner can benefit from vocational education, nor that all slow learners can do so. Too often school administrators and teachers welcome the development of a program of vocational education because it offers a convenient place to shunt students who are not doing well in the traditional studies of the school curriculum and they find this easier than to reform the traditional practices in ways which will meet the needs of individual students. This results in having many young people enrolled in vocational programs for the wrong reasons and at the wrong stage of their education.

Vocational Education and the Unmotivated Student

Some students who are not slow learners—who may indeed be potentially superior students—do not fit into the limited academic mold which is the only program that many schools offer. There are as many school dropouts among the bright as among the dull. These students, for a variety of reasons, have no strong desire to make good in school, and they baffle and annoy their teachers even though they may not always become discipline problems. To many administrators vocational education seems to be the answer for them, probably because it is the only avaliable alternative. Yet there is no reason to believe that a student who finds no interest in academic or general studies will be motivated by the opportunity to follow a vocational course. Studies of school retention show rates no higher, and often significantly lower, for vocational students than for those in academic and college entrance programs.[16, 17, 18]

Only when a student has settled upon an occupational goal and is determined to reach it will he demonstrate real motivation in preparing for it. When this occurs, occupational education can become the means for expressing a life purpose and achieving it, but as we have seen this is a decision-making process which cannot be forced and which is highly individual in its nature and in its timing. All the evidence shows that only occasionally is an unmotivated student stimulated by vocational education to achieve better or to remain longer in school.

Educating for a Changing Occupational Life

A generation ago, and long before that, it was customary for most workers to enter an occupation in their youth, and, if they found it agreeable, to remain in it during their working lifetime. One might have to change jobs or employers, but seldom occupations. A useful occupation, once learned, could be counted upon to provide a livelihood as long as a man was likely to work, because changes in most occupations came slowly and did not disrupt the character of the work done during the ordinary span of working years. All this is changing rapidly. We are living in a time when the always accelerating pace of technological change is able to alter completely the nature of an occupation within the space of a few years. The changes may, in fact, eliminate the occupation entirely, forcing workers to seek jobs of another type. More often the result is a drastic reduction in the numbers of people needed, as in the field of agriculture. Economists predict that in the future, workers may be required to enter a new occupation not once, but several times during their working lifetime.

This will bring at least three important demands to occupational education of the future. One is to offer what may be called conversion education to large numbers of workers at all times. This service would be designed to help the worker each time it becomes necessary for him to make an occupational change. It must be readily and quickly available to him when he needs it, and sufficiently intensive so that he may be back at work in the new occupation as soon as possible.

A second need will be for more extensive assistance to those whose continued employment depends upon updating their skills and knowledge to satisfy the changes in their own occupations. This form of training, supplementary to the job, has always been a part of vocational education, but the future will call for much more of it. Complete cooperation and coordination with employers and with organized labor are essential if supplementary education of this kind is to be successful.

There is a third and more fundamental objective, however, which must be emphasized in occupational education if it is to prepare our citizens adequately for a changing world of work. This is to educate youth to expect and accept change in their occupational lives—to know that their first occupation may not be their last and that to change occupations is a normal and often necessary event in our technological society. Too much of vocational education has been conducted on the assumption that the student will always remain in the occupation he has learned in school. Adjustability to occupational change demands a greater emphasis upon general education, since general intellectual and social skills are the most transferable to differing occupations.[19] Part of an occupational education should help the learner to understand that occupational conversion education will be available to him when he needs it, that he is entitled to it, and that it should be regarded as part of his educational life, similar to his elementary, secondary, and other formal education.

Summary

Vocational education has usually been thought of as something that begins when general education has been completed and when the student has made a final career choice. This concept is too limited to be useful in the future. Occupational education must begin much earlier, must include learning about the world of work, and must take responsibility for guiding and assisting youth in the long process of choosing a vocation. This will result in teaching and learning about the world of work beginning in the early grades and continuing throughout most of the secondary school years. Only then will actual preparation for an occupation be attempted. This is a relatively new idea, unfamiliar to both general and vocational educators, and no instructional framework now exists for it. All of the curricular and instructional planning for this very necessary task remains to be done.

Most vocational educators have assumed that students for their courses could and should be selected on the basis of their potential for success in the occupation being taught. They have relied upon aptitude tests, interest inventories, personality traits and indicators of general scholastic ability to determine suitability for training. We now know that there are no reliable means for predicting aptitudes or potential for particular occupations, and that the process of vocational choice is a long and complex one. We are also beginning to understand that the lack of knowledge about individual and occupational characteristics and the lack of confidence in long range projections make the role of the vocational counselor a modest one.

The slow learner is often an early candidate for occupational education because his slower pace of learning puts him behind in the academic studies. Yet this is a poor reason for encouraging him to follow a vocational program. On the other hand, slow learners can, and ultimately will, find and follow a wage earning occupation, and since vocational education has certain features which are well adapted to their slower pace of learning it has a responsibility for accepting and educating them.

Motivation toward learning is a complex matter and the theory that occupational education will somehow motivate the disinterested or alienated student is a doubtful one. The desire to learn springs from the conviction that the learning will lead to some desired individual goal. Vocational education can be attractive only to those whose career goals are well formulated and when the probability is high that it will lead to a job in the chosen field of work. There is a frequent assumption, but little evidence, that vocational education, as presently conducted, meets these requirements for many students.

The changing nature of occupational life calls for much occupational adaptability on the part of future workers. They must expect to be more or less continually in the process of renewing their skills and updating their knowledge, and they must be prepared at times to learn new occupations. Occupational education will fail them badly if it does not educate them to understand this and if it neglects to provide the programs for skill renewal and for learning the new occupations.

REFERENCES

1. University of California at Los Angeles, Division of Vocational Education. *A Guide for the Development of Curriculum in Vocational and Technical Education.* Los Angeles: University of California, 1969.
2. Massachusetts Institute of Technology. *Report of the Summer Study on Occupational, Vocational and Technical Education.*
3. Feldman, Marvin. "Zeroing in on a Program of Zero Rejects." *School Shop* 29, no. 8 (April, 1970) : 86 ff.
4. Leighbody. "Impact of the Area Vocational School." *Educational Leadership.*
5. Ginzberg. *Vocational Education.*
6. Peters, Herman J., and Hansen, J. C., eds. *Vocational Guidance and Career Development: Selected Readings.* New York: Macmillan Co., 1966.
7. Brookover and Nosow. "A Sociological Analysis of Vocational Education in the United States." *Education for a Changing World of Work.*
8. Barlow, Melvin, ed., *Vocational Education.* National Association for the Study of Education, Sixty-Fourth Yearbook. Chicago: University of Chicago Press, 1965.
9. Kaufman, Jacob, and Lewis, M. *The Potential of Vocational Education.* The Institute of Research on Human Resources. University Park, Penn.: The Pennsylvania State University, 1968.
10. Massachusetts Institute of Technology. *Report of the Summer Study on Occupational, Vocational and Technical Education.*
11. Crites, John O. "Appraising the Appraisal Instruments." *American Vocational Journal* 43, no. 9 (December, 1968) : 22 ff.
12. The Brookings Institution. *Vocational Education.* Supplement to the *Journal of Human Resources*, vol. 3. Madison: University of Wisconsin Press, 1968.
13. United States Department of Labor, Manpower Administration, Bureau of Employment Security. *Manual for the General Aptitude Test Battery, Section 3, Development.* Washington, D. C.: U. S. Dept. of Labor, 1967.
14. Eninger. *The Process and the Product of T and I Vocational Educational Education in the United States.*
15. Arnow, Philip. "Bridging the Gap from School to Work." *Occupational Outlook Quarterly* 12, no. 12 (December, 1968).
16. Staff report on vocational education presented to the Board of Education. Mimeographed. Buffalo, N. Y.: Board of Education (March, 1967).

17. Kohler, Mary C. *Youth and Work in New York City.* New York: The Taconic Foundation, 1960.
18. The Brookings Institution. *Vocational Education,* p. 81.
19. Leighbody, Gerald. "Vocational Education Looks to the Future." *Influences in Curriculum Change.* Washington, D. C.: Association for Supervision and Curriculum Development, 1968.

CHAPTER 4

THE VOCATIONAL CURRICULUM AND THE WORLD OF WORK

The Vocational Curriculum and Program Goals

The curriculum of occupational education, like other curriculums, reflects what the curriculum planners perceive to be the major goals of the program. A curriculum consists of the learning experiences which are presumed to help the learner accomplish the accepted and desired purposes of this program. Therefore, as these purposes change, and perhaps broaden in scope and shift in priorities in response to changing social needs, it is reasonable to expect corresponding changes in the curriculum. Indeed, the modern curriculum is dynamic and growing, not a static means by which the school educates the young.

Throughout its history in the United States vocational education has been directed largely toward a single aim—to produce trained manpower for the benefit of the nation and the individual being trained. Furthermore, it has concentrated its effort upon a limited number of occupations, chiefly the agricultural and skilled industrial occupations for boys, and homemaking activities and office occupations for girls. In recent years some attention has been paid to the distributive and service areas of employment, including the health occupations, but these have received far less emphasis than they should command in view of their now dominant role in the economy. In each area, however, the major resources have been used to reach students in the secondary schools and to prepare them for immediate employment in a well defined job.

So long as this remained the first and foremost goal of occupational education, the task of curriculum development was not difficult to plan or to accomplish. Essentially it resolved itself into three steps. First, the occupation to be learned was analyzed and studied in order to identify the skills and processes which the worker must perform in order to practice the occupation. Second, further analysis was made to identify the directly related items of theory and technical information which the worker would need so that he could apply the skills and processes successfully. And third, both skills and related knowledge were arranged in a learning sequence which began with the more elementary and simple elements and progressed to the more difficult and complex. This method of curriculum construction, known as trade or occupational analysis, was for many years taught to all vocational teachers and curriculum makers as the basis for most vocational curriculum development.[1] No attempt was made, under this plan, to consider the relation of general or academic learnings to vocational needs, or to integrate any parts of general education with those that were strictly vocational. The occupational analysis approach is a useful and effective method for planning those aspects of the vocational curriculum which deal with the specialized techniques of an occupation, and while the curriculum must include such content, it is, by itself, far from adequate for modern occupational education.

The curriculum for occupational education must relate to goals which are much broader than those of training the student to become a worker in a particular job. Venn, in his study of vocational and technical education, has emphasized that vocational education is much more than just the acquisition of skills.[2] Unfortunately, vocational educators have sometimes stressed this objective so much that it has appeared to many to be the only purpose of the program.

The curriculum for occupational education must aim for goals which go much beyond getting someone ready for a payroll job. It should be designed to equip all youth and adults for successful living and earning and learning in a society which is already dominated by a technological explosion, for their own benefit and for the welfare of that society. Unless they are prepared to cope with the social, economic and political changes which are bound to come, by understanding the technological forces which produce them, knowing how to perform some job which is presently available will be of very brief value indeed. Vocational curriculum planners, like those who plan other areas of the curriculum, need to start with basic educational decisions which are supported by research evidence and which lead to sound educational policies. Such decisions should take account of at least four major determinants. These are the nature and needs of society, the nature and needs of the learner, the nature of the learning process, and the role and function of the teacher.[3] Occupational education has, of course a special concern for the manpower needs of society, but to respond to these only in terms of supplying a labor market is a mistake. Neither should the other educational needs of the learner be subordinated to his need for becoming a competent worker. Those who develop vocational curriculums should apply the same principles as those who plan all other curriculum areas of the total educational program, and adapt those principles toward helping people achieve useful, satisfying work lives.[4]

The preparation and production of instructional materials should not be confused with curriculum planning for vocational education. Curriculum planning is the fundamental responsibility of the vocational educator, not the production of teaching materials, although the resourceful teacher will often create special materials of his own to improve his teaching. For the most part, however, instructional materials are best produced commercially by publishers and others who are equipped and qualified to do so. Publishers need, and seek, the advice and help of vocational educators in deciding what kinds of instructional materials are needed for curriculum purposes, but there is no justification for establishing, with public funds, projects for writing and producing instructional materials in competition with private publishers. The Vocational Amendments Act of 1968 authorizes, for the first time, substantial amounts of money for vocational curriculum research and development.[5] This is a much needed and very valuable addition to vocational education funding, but it should not be put to such uses as printing and distributing teaching materials. These funds should be allocated to curriculum planning, research and revision in its broadest sense, while experienced professional publishers are relied upon to furnish the materials needed to support the curriculums which the vocational educators decide upon.

Curriculum cannot be separated from instruction, and therefore from teachers, nor should it be. It has long been customary for vocational teachers to be active in curriculum development, often because they were the only experts in the subjects they taught. More recently, all teachers have taken a renewed interest in curriculum decision making, and teacher organizations, in negotiating contracts with their employers, frequently demand more active participation in planning the school program and curriculums, rather than limiting their interest to financial matters alone.

Curriculum decisions made by so-called curriculum experts and passed along to teachers to be followed have seldom found their way into classroom action. The only curriculum a teacher is likely to take seriously is one that he has helped to plan, and the more competent and professional the teacher the more this will be true. Vocational funds spent to improve instruction through curriculum development will have little effect unless the teacher has a leading part in the process of curriculum planning. This means that curriculum improvement must be closely coordinated with teacher education, and this will require greater professionalization and broader training for vocational teachers. In addition to their occupational skills, vocational teachers in the future will need more emphasis on other professional competencies and a better balance between occupational, general liberal and professional knowledge in their preparation for teaching.

Technology and Occupational Change

The influence of technology upon the stability of occupational life has already been referred to. In addition to this, however, the ever accelerating impact of technology creates many economic and social changes which affect every segment of American life, and what has already happened is but a prelude to greater changes to come. In the realm of occupational education the effects of technology have brought changes which the vocational curriculum has yet to respond to, even while the need for other changes has already appeared. In some respects the demands of technology seem to be of a new order, but what is really new is not the fact that technology mandates change, but that the changes brought by modern technology are so swift and so continuous. The past quarter century in particular has been a period of unprecedented breakthroughs in technical knowledge and its application to human affairs. Among these are:

The energy breakthrough. When the means for releasing the energy of the atom were achieved, man gained access to a new source of energy which is theoretically unlimited. The possibilities for using this new energy are just beginning to be understood. Our experience with this new technology is very short, but although it emerged as a weapon, already it is serving enough useful purposes to suggest something of its tremendous beneficial potential for the future.

The health breakthrough. The conquest of disease has made such rapid strides that the life span of the American people has been significantly lengthened in recent years. The combined knowledge from a number of technologies which has improved health and lengthened life has also brought new social and political demands for universal health care, and one result is the appearance of several new health related occupations and a greatly increased need for workers in all the fields of health.

The production breakthrough. New applications of several technologies, in combinations which are often referred to as automation, have brought a whole new dimension to the capacity of the economy to produce goods and food. A production explosion has occurred in agriculture and in manufacturing, with profound consequences for those who work in both.

The knowledge breakthrough. The introduction and continuous refinement of the computer has brought about a revolution in our capacity to manage and process information and data and for testing observed experimental data for relationships and meaning. This has made it possible to telescope into a few years the recording, classifying and storing of amounts of new knowledge which would formerly have required several decades to acquire. Since a major part of business activity and of scientific research consists of recording and processing data, an enormous expansion in these areas has been possible, with a relatively small increase in manpower.[6]

The communications breakthrough. One of the most dramatic effects of the electronic age has occurred in the field of communications. Whole new galaxies of occupations have emerged from this development, a development in which intercontinental telecasts of good quality, via satellite, are now commonplace, and very successful telecasts from the moon have been demonstrated.

The breakthrough in space. The tremendous achievements in space exploration, including the moon landings, have been made possible by the employment of very advanced and exotic technical accomplishments. Some of these have already found their way into use for other purposes which promise great benefits to mankind, and the transfer of knowledge from space technology to other useful applications has scarcely begun.

Other breakthroughs could be described, and still others may be expected. Those which have been mentioned, however, illustrate two highly important characteristics of technological change which inevitably influence occupations, and therefore occupational education and its curriculum.

1. Technology has a built-in acceleration factor. Each new discovery and development comes more quickly than the last, and the time from the discovery of a new technique to its widespread adoption and use grows constantly shorter. The modern practice of concentrating great resources on single research and development projects accounts in part for this.

2. Knowledge is irreversible. Like energy, it cannot be destroyed, and new knowledge always leads to more.

The technology which so predominates our culture produces not only important changes in the nature of occupations, but also in the distribution of occupations within the work force. For the vocational curriculum planner, nothing could be more important than to recognize and take account of this fact. Yet the program of occupational education in the schools has been slow to do so, and has continued to enroll the majority of students in curriculums devoted to occupations with static or declining manpower needs while often failing to respond sufficiently to needs in areas of greater growth. Some of the broad changes which result from the great technological breakthroughs, and which must be reflected in the curriculums of occupational education are these:

1. More goods are produced for more consumers, but with a smaller and smaller portion of the work force required to produce them. However, those who are thus employed must be better educated and must possess more sophisticated skills and knowledge than their predecessors.

2. More food and fiber is produced and more people are better fed and clothed by fewer and fewer farmers. The percentage of the work force engaged in farming has dropped from more than forty percent in the early part of the century to about five percent at the present time. Workers continue to be forced off the land while the quantity of agricultural products continues to increase. But those who remain and those who will be needed in the future require much greater knowledge of scientific agriculture, coupled with business skills and training.

3. Nearly all jobs call for a higher level of education for entry than they formerly did, and a longer period of general education prior to occupational specialization. At one time a full high school education was achieved by only a small number of Americans. Today it is hardly sufficient for a decent job, and very large numbers of people are continuing their education beyond it.

4. The need for manual skills in most jobs is decreasing, while cognitive, social, and interpersonal skills are more and more in demand. Jobs which call for manual skills are still to be found, but it is in the nature of modern technology to cause them to decline in number. Arnstein, who has studied this trend and prepared a report on automation and its effects on education for the National Education Association, has pointed out how machines are making craftsmanship obsolete and radically changing the nature of skills.[7]

5. Already more people are employed in providing services for other people than in producing goods and food for them. Two-thirds of the work force is now engaged in what may be broadly classified as service occupations, including those in government, while we are fed and housed and provided with an endless variety of manufactured goods by the other third. This is a remarkable reversal of the distribution of occupations from the time when the first programs of vocational education were established.

6. In addition to the shift in the distribution of jobs, as technology advances it creates wholly new jobs and categories of jobs, and these too tend to demand better educated and better trained workers. Computer programmers, air traffic controllers, environmental control specialists are a few among a great many new occupations which were either non-existent or rarely found a quarter century ago. In drafting the Vocational Education Amendments Act of 1968 the Congress showed its awareness that many new and unusual occupations are emerging in the economy, by providing that some of the funds for vocational curriculum development should be used to prepare for them.

Keeping the Vocational Curriculum Updated

If the vocational curriculum is to be continuously valid it must necessarily undergo changes which are at least equivalent to those that have actually occurred in the society and in the economy. But vocational curriculum planners need to do more than this. They need to assess carefully the major directions of change and plan for the different world of work which these trends will lead to, and not react with stubborn resistance until change is forced upon them. If, for example, one of the effects of technological change is to postpone, for most youth, specialized job training until after they have completed high school, this should be accepted and planned for, not ignored or opposed, in developing the curriculums for programs now being planned. This kind of thinking calls for what Charles Kettering speaks of as the tomorrow mind instead of the yesterday mind.[8]

Keeping the curriculum updated has always presented problems to vocational educators. The problems they have sought to meet have been those growing out of the goals they were attempting to reach, and, because of their concentration on occupational specialization, keeping up to date has generally meant trying to incorporate into the instructional program whatever new techniques might appear in factory, office, or on the farm. To do this successfully has usually required the acquisition of new, different, and often expensive equipment as well as other costly changes which industry and business can afford but which schools as a rule cannot. The vocational educator, therefore, in his effort to keep up with the changing technology, has often been frustrated and left behind because, to him, updating has been an attempt to match industry's progress, technique by technique and process by process. Whether this will ever be possible, except in unusual cases, may be questioned. A more fundamental question is whether it is a sound approach to vocational curriculum planning, in view of current technological trends. This subject is dealt with in a report resulting from one of the most significant studies of curriculum purposes to be made in recent years, a study which was conducted by the Department of Education of the Province of Ontario, Canada. In discussing the question as to how the schools can provide students with skills that will match the changing requirements of the work world, the report concludes that the schools cannot hope to do this because the needs of the labor market cannot be forecast to this extent.[9]

It may be more important to keep the vocational curriculum updated by making educational decisions of a much broader nature than those which try to take account of each new development in every occupation. For example, vocational curriculum makers ought to consider such changes as the following, all of which are suggested by the present trends in the occupational world:

Shifting from the predominantly craft and agricultural occupations which now occupy so much attention in the program to the service occupations for the majority of students enrolled. As recently as 1968 the report of the ad hoc Advisory Committee on Vocational Education stated that of all students registered in trade and industrial courses, sixty percent were to be found in three trades—machine shop, auto mechanics and drafting.[10] This is but one example of a curriculum imbalance which needs correcting.

Building curriculums which prepare for general categories of occupations rather than concentrating on teaching the techniques of particular occupations.

Introducing a much stronger component of general education, integrated with occupational studies, and including effective education in career planning and choosing.

Eliminating consideration of the traditional service areas (such as trade and industrial, agricultural, homemaking) which have formed the structural framework of the vocational

program since 1917, and developing curriculums without regard to these outworn service categories which have so often
compartmentalized the vocational curriculum.

Planning more and more of the vocational curriculum for
the post secondary period rather than for the high school.

Directing the curriculum toward the development of occupationally adaptable individuals, prepared for a lifetime of
learning and a lifetime of occupational change.

The Range of Occupations and the Vocational Curriculum

Spokesmen for vocational education have often talked as if
its eventual task is to train workers for all, or most of the occupations in the economy. Snedden was one of the early writers
who apparently thought in these terms. He proposed a scheme
which would provide organized vocational training for vir-
tually all workers, and which included the establishment of
training centers to serve a region, or even an entire state, for
those occupations which require relatively few workers. Those
desiring such training would attend such centers on a residen-
tial basis, returning to their own communities to practice their
occupations when their training was completed. His plans even
included the training of railroad workers for the entire railroad industry by setting up a center using a few miles of track,
locomotives and other equipment.[11]

Present-day vocational educators would probably consider
this impractical, but suggestions are still being made as to
the scope of the vocational curriculum which, if seriously undertaken, would present impossible problems, and, what is
more important, are quite unrealistic and unnecessary in the
vast and complex labor market of this country. As recently as
1969 the *American Vocational Journal* carried the statement
that vocational education now has the responsibility for occupational education for all persons who do not earn a baccalaureate degree.[12] Other claims have been made that since only
twenty percent of our students do complete a baccalaureate
degree, all of the rest should be pursuing a vocational program.
This can only mean that they envision eighty percent of all
youth becoming vocational students. Those who express such
ideas have not thought through some of the assumptions on
which they are based, for underlying any such expansion of
vocational educational services would require a form of educa-

tional and occupational predestination which cannot exist in a free society with a free labor market. How are we to know in advance, for example, who will finally earn a baccalaureate degree and who will not, or who will terminate his formal education at what point? Should those who enter college programs without completing them have been denied the opportunity to try? We cannot, of course, know the educational or career future of any individual during his early years, but even if we could, we would surely not wish to limit or deny his individual right to choose or to aspire to advanced education. If all but the degree earners should have to look to formal vocational education for their occupational preparation, the vocational curriculum would have to include literally thousands of different occupations, and prepare teachers in an equal number of specialities. This is obviously neither possible nor desirable.

Of the more than seventy million persons who now constitute the American work force, not more than ten or fifteen percent have learned their occupations in school. Yet the nation's work is done, and done well, in an economy which is perhaps the most productive in the world. Clearly, the majority of those who work must learn their occupations on the job, supported by the general education which the schools can give ·them. The occupational specializations needed to sustain our highly technological economy are so many and so diverse that efforts to make the schools responsible for teaching most of them are unreasonable and unnecessary.

Learning in School and on the Job

Once this is recognized, the next task of the curriculum maker is to determine which aspects of occupational life are best learned on the job and which can better be learned in school. There is at least one respect in which the schools should serve all youth, regardless of how advanced their future education may become, in helping them prepare for work, and this is to include career planning and decision making in the curriculum. Grant Venn has pointed out that the schools will also have to assume another responsibility which goes well beyond what they now consider to be their function. This is to form educational partnerships with the three principal employing agencies in our society—business, industry, and government—and then become responsible for having every student who leaves school enter some program of further education or secure a job in which he can begin to learn an occupation.[13] The transition from school to work is becoming so difficult for most young people that some agency must accept the task of helping those who do not readily find their own way to cross the bridge between school and work.

In order to do this, funds which would otherwise be spent in trying to offer all vocational training in the schools could legitimately be used to compensate private employers for the lower initial productivity of the learner, and for other costs of training, or added to the budgets of government agencies which accept and train those emerging from the schools. This is already being done under provisions for on the job training under the Manpower Development and Training Act, and could be widely extended.[14]

The Vocational Curriculum and the General Curriculum

Vocational curriculum planning cannot proceed as if it had no relationship to the general curriculum. Vocational education is just a part of the total education of the individual, and it cannot function as something separate from the rest of his education. The vocational curriculum should be planned with the assistance of those who work in the academic areas of the school program in order to assure that the student will benefit fully from a well rounded education.

Even though certain general competencies have not, in the past, been thought of as belonging within the curriculum of occupational education, they must now be so regarded, because getting and holding a job depends upon them. Jobs of all kinds and at all levels now demand the use of reading skills, of written and oral expression, and certain mathematical skills as minimums. Social and human relation skills are essential for success in more and more occupations, as team and task force approaches to work assignments are now frequently employed. Therefore vocational educators must include these types of skills in their curriculums.[15]

Summary

Every curriculum is a reflection of the philosophy of those who create it and bespeaks the program goals which they most value. So long as vocational education limited its goals to the teaching of techniques of particular occupations, the occupational analysis method for deriving curriculum content was adequate. Some use can still be made of it, but vocational education must now be prepared to take on broader, multipurpose responsibilities, and therefore must broaden and extend its curriculum. Among its additional objectives must be those of career planning and choosing, of preparing workers for lives of occupational change, and of responding to the new economic and social changes through which onrushing technology is altering the world of work. It will have to satisfy occupational needs for better educated and more occupationally sophisticated workers in jobs which will require higher levels of education for entry and for continued employment, and with a greater emphasis upon occupations other than those in industry, manufacturing and agriculture. Concentration will have to be upon the new kinds of generalized skills which are needed in a service oriented job market rather than upon the manual skills of the past. Much of the program of occupational education in the future will take place under the auspices of the school, but outside the walls of the school building, and the school will need to assume the responsibility for having every student move to the next higher level of education or to a learning situation in a wage earning job.

<h2 style="text-align:center">REFERENCES</h2>

1. Selvidge, Robert, and Fryklund, Verne. *Principles of Trade and Industrial Teaching*. Peoria, Ill.: Manual Arts Press, 1930.
2. Venn. *Man, Education and Work*.
3. University of California at Los Angeles, Division of Vocational Education. *A Guide for the Development of Curriculum in Vocational and Technical Education*.
4. Taba, Hilda. *Curriculum Development: Theory and Practice*. New York: Harcourt, Brace and World, 1962.
5. U. S. Congress. *Vocational Education Amendments Act*.
6. Frank, Nathaniel H. "The Computer and Society." *The New York Times*, Special Supplement (April 24, 1966).
7. Arnstein, George E. *The Bulletin of the National Association of Secondary School Principals* (November, 1964).
8. Boyd, Thomas A. *Professional Amateur: The Biography of Charles E. Kettering*. New York: E. P. Dutton Company, 1957.
9. Provincial Committee on Aims and Objectives of Education in the Schools of Ontario. *Living and Learning*. Toronto: Ontario Department of Education, 1968.
10. Advisory Council on Vocational Education. *Vocational Education: The Bridge Between Man and His Work*.

11. Snedden. *Vocational Education.*
12. Burkett. "Latest Word from Washington." *American Vocational Journal* 44, no. 1 (January, 1969) : 5-6.
13. Venn, Grant. Unpublished address presented to the American Technical Education Association. Niagara Falls, N. Y. (November, 1967).
14. U. S. Congress. *Manpower Development and Training Act of 1962.* Public Law 87-415, 87th Cong., 1962. Amendments by Public Laws 88-214 and 89-15, 1963 & 1965.
15. University of California at Los Angeles, Division of Vocational Education. *A Guide for the Development of Curriculum in Vocational and Technical Education.*

CHAPTER 5

VOCATIONAL EDUCATION AND
GENERAL EDUCATION IN THE
MODERN AGE

The Historic Issue

There is probably no educational issue that has been so long debated and so little understood as that of the relationship between vocational and general education. It has been discussed in terms of the liberal vs the utilitarian studies, cultural vs practical education, academic vs vocational education, and general vs specialized education. It is interesting to observe that the usual assumption has been that a choice must be made between one or the other, and upon this premise strong philosophical disagreements have arisen between those who favor vocational education and those who believe that only the liberal studies are educative. One of the few who have been able to see the weaknesses in both positions has been the British philosopher Whitehead, who, in his lecture on technical education suggested that there can be no truly liberal education which is not technical and no truly technical education which is not liberal.[1]

As we have learned from reviewing the way in which vocational education developed in America, its proponents have put much emphasis upon its utilitarian, job functioning values and have tended to hold academic studies and the humanities in somewhat low regard. In the preparation of vocational teachers and leaders the liberal studies have often been replaced with the technical, leaving them with an imbalance in their education which has tended to set them apart from the larger educational world. On the other hand, the generalist is often deficient in any understanding of the technological areas of knowledge and of technology as a force in the lives of men. { He therefore sees occupational education as having narrow goals and short term values, and he questions its place in the educational scheme.)

The time is now past when that which is vocational and that which is general or liberal can be identified separately and treated as different kinds of education for different groups of people. Whatever philosophical grounds may have existed formerly for such a distinction have been obliterated by modern technology and its effects. Increasingly the technical skills which make possible the performance of particular jobs are impossible to identify from other life skills which are the product of general learnings and which are equally essential for job success. This is the nature of work and of jobs in the modern age.

Preparation For Job Entry

Occupational education has been much preoccupied with the preparation of the young for specific payroll jobs and with their subsequent entry into those jobs. While it has always tried to serve the employed worker in order to help him increase and extend his skills, its chief concern has been with pre-employment training for immediate employment. The best evidence of this is the manner in which vocational educators have chosen to evaluate the success of their programs. Invariably the measure used is the extent to which students are placed in the jobs for which they are trained. Most of the official studies which have been of the programs of vocational education in the schools have used this as their yardstick, and the report issued by the Panel of Consultants on Vocational Education following their 1961 national study contains the statement that the acid test of the success of vocational education is the extent to which its graduates are placed in the jobs for which they were trained.[2] The Eninger study of high school Trade and Industrial Education of 1965 was based upon this assumption[3] and the later study by Kaufman and Schaefer used the same kind of data as a principal criterion for evaluation.[4]

By restricting the evaluative criteria of occupational education so largely to that of job entry into a specific occupation, the program as a whole necessarily becomes narrow in its scope.[5] Additionally, most of the follow-up studies of vocational graduates, whether national, regional or local show that the percentage of vocational graduates who find jobs in the exact occupation for which they trained averages only about thirty percent. This figure is much higher in certain categories of jobs, and correspondingly much lower in others. This leaves about seventy percent who do not meet the test applied by vocational educators to their own programs. There is no recognized standard with which this degree of placement success can be judged in order to estimate whether it represents a good, fair or poor result. To many, however, it seems very modest, and it brings the efficiency of the program, at least at the high school level, into question.

In order to present a more favorable and perhaps a fairer picture of their achievements, vocational educators have introduced the concept of placement in related occupations as being legitimate to include in placement records. It is relatively easy to know whether a graduate is employed directly in the occupation for which he trained, but if he is found in another occupation there is the problem deciding whether or not it is related. There is no common definition or specification for identifying relatedness and therefore its definition can become very loose indeed. By using this concept, however poorly defined, some studies have been able to show that approximately fifty percent of vocational graduates are employed in the occupations for which they were trained or in a related occupation.[6] Even this would not seem to be a very high level of accomplishment for the program to achieve.

The effort to maximize the number of job placements has tended to narrow the occupational target for the vocational student and to direct his curriculum toward a higher degree of specialization. It has also caused vocational educators to believe that in order to prepare a student adequately a large amount of his time in school must be spent in learning job techniques. Both of these policies reduce the amount of general education which the student can receive, and even if the goal of immediate job entry is achieved it is at the expense of his broader, long-term opportunities.[7]

It is time to re-examine the emphasis upon job placement

and first job needs as the most important goal of occupational education. Other priorities must be considered in justifying, conducting and evaluating the program. What is needed is a broader set of goals which, taken together, will help people to reach and enjoy a better quality of occupational life in a high technology culture, where the earning of a paycheck is but one of the goals to be sought.

Preparation For a Career

Concentrating upon first job preparation has increased the focus of occupational education upon supplying local labor markets and local employers with beginning workers, and to this extent it has lessened the efforts of the school to prepare youth for a career rather than for an entry job. Too much of the student's time is demanded for the learning of applied practical skills, particularly in the high school, thereby de-emphasizing and leaving too little time for the general studies which are so necessary for his later development and for his progress up the career ladder. This has been noted and commented upon by observers like Congressman Pucinski who have become familiar with the nature of the present program.[8] To secure one's first job is important, but a high degree of specialization in the vocational curriculum is not needed for successful placement, and it is the broadly prepared worker, not the narrowly trained specialist who has the best chance for career growth and occupational continuity.

We have observed in reviewing the history of vocational education that there has long existed a feeling by many vocational educators that their programs are regarded as educationally inferior and as less than first-rate education. They have often charged this to prejudice by parents, students and other educators toward those who "work with their hands," and as recently as 1969 the first report of the new National Advisory Council on Vocational Education accused the American public of intellectual snobbery in its attitude toward vocational education.[9] This problem will be discussed more fully in Chapter 9, but at this point it must be noted that one of the reasons why many parents reject vocational education for their children is not because of snobbish prejudice but because they fear that to enroll in a vocational curriculum will cut them off from further education and deprive them of future educational and career opportunities. As vocational education has operated in the past this has unfortunately been too often true. It has been planned as terminal education, culminating in a job rather than a career. Many vocational educators have been aware of this and accordingly they have been as reluctant as other parents to encourage their own children to pursue a vocational curriculum in securing their education.

Venn believes that one answer is to credit learning which is not academic toward admission to post high school programs.[10] Yet there is little possibility of this so long as occupational education remains as a form of highly specialized training for an entry job instead of an open-ended education for a career.

There is no reason to believe that broadening the vocational curriculum to include general education objectives will result in watering down or abandoning the vocational outcomes, as some vocationalists seem to fear. On the contrary, it will make occupational education more effective and more compatible with education as a whole and will open many more career doors for students who elect to follow it.

What Employers Expect of the Schools

The idea that employers generally desire the schools to train students to perform the exact skills needed in particular jobs has never been borne out by actual experience. There are some exceptions to this, as in certain office occupations, where the employer does expect the school to develop typing skills up to a certain minimum of speed and accuracy. Yet those who hire graduates of business programs complain more often of deficiencies in spelling, grammar and punctuation than in typing. For the most part employers are less interested in the specialized skills which a beginning worker may possess than vocational educators usually assume and the study by Kaufman and Schaefer revealed this quite clearly. In this study data were secured from more than six hundred employers and first line supervisors and the majority reported that they gave no employment preference to vocational graduates on the basis of their high school vocational studies. They employed both academic and vocational graduates with equal readiness for many of the same jobs if the applicants had good attitudes

toward work, good work habits and a willingness to be taught
and to respond to supervision. Graduates from both academic
and vocational curriculums who were hired proved satisfactory
as employees as evaluated by their employers.[11]

There are certain licensed occupations which cannot be
practiced without formal in-school training leading to a license
—such as cosmetology or nursing—and in such cases the employer can hire only those who have completed an approved
course. Yet even then he is likely to prefer those qualified
students who have more general education and a broad rather
than a narrow occupational preparation.[12]

Admiral Charles Horne, President of the General Dynamics
Corporation, is one of many employers who have expressed a
preference for the broadly educated worker. When called upon
at a recent vocational education conference to comment upon
what industry expects of the schools in preparing youth for
the world of work he responded that what industry wants is
a youngster who has been educated to think and to apply his
thinking, who has been educated to understand what is going
on around him, and who knows how to communicate.[13]

All the available evidence suggests that it is not necessary
for occupational education to emphasize specialized work skills
at the expense of general education in order to satisfy the expectations of employers. On the contrary, in an advanced
technological society, the most salable skills are likely to be
those which are non-specialized and which are achieved
through a sound general education. These are the skills that
make an individual adaptable and which are most useful in
a variety of occupations.

Balancing Breadth and Specialization

To achieve an appropriate balance between breadth and
depth specialization has long been one of the more difficult
problems of education. An education which results in knowing
a little about a great many things may produce only a shallow,
superficial dilettante, while knowing a great deal about a
narrow field results in an equally unbalanced and deficient
education. The tendency of vocational education has been to
teach for a particular occupation, and breadth has been defined as the extent to which all details of that occupation have
been included, but this kind of occupational education is no

longer meaningful. It must be re-designed to embrace everything that will help an individual to learn his own talents, to evaluate them in relation to his career plans, and to develop them usefully for occupational success.[14]

Technology has vastly increased the number of occupational specialties in our economy and most of these in turn have become increasingly complex. Yet, paradoxically, it has also created the need for broadly trained and educated workers rather than the limited specialist in the work force. Intellectual skills are becoming more important than performance skills in the world of work, and occupational education, to be successful, must adopt the changes which this implies. Certain subjects and studies which have never been really essential as a part of occupational education have now become so because the capabilities which they produce are now necessary in order to secure and hold a job.

The Theory of the Segmented Individual

Much of the occupational education in the schools has been organized as if the student had two separate and distinct sets of educational needs, with little relationship between them—one set for his vocational life and the other set for all other aspects of living. When offered in a separate vocational school the program has often functioned as two schools within a school, and too often something of the same atmosphere is to be found in the comprehensive high school. The student's day is divided into two parts, so that he studies vocational skills during one part of the day and becomes an academic student for the rest of the time. In the area vocational schools, which have become popular throughout the country, the break is even sharper, for the high school student spends half his day at his home school where he receives general education and the other half at an area skill center which teaches occupational skills to the students from a number of feeder high schools.

In both situations the student is treated as though, for educational purposes, he has become a segmented individual. His general education studies have little or no relation to his vocational interests or training in the eyes of either his academic or his vocational teachers. Where the area school exists the two groups of teachers seldom, perhaps never, meet each other. In the two-year colleges having occupational departments the teachers of occupational skills often identify themselves only partially with the general education program and its teachers. There is a tendency for both groups of teachers to behave as though each was responsible for only a part of the student's education and as though each part stood alone in the process of educating the student. This is what the 1968 report of the Advisory Council on Vocational Education meant when it said that, "The current status of occupational education is clouded by an unfortunate tendency to consider vocational and general education as incompatible."[15]

The concept of the segmented learner is, of course, unsupported by anything we know about the learning process and is, in fact quite at variance with modern learning theory. Realistically it is impossible to compartmentalize education into components labeled vocational, general, academic or cultural, and any attempt to do so produces a fragmented and inferior education. Especially in a society where technology can accomplish every task except reflective thinking and humane decision making, the human worker must, through his education, be prepared to apply to his work life those intellectual and value based skills which no machine can ever possess. To redirect occupational education in these terms is not to abandon skill development as a major purpose in preparing for work. Rather it is to acknowledge that in today's world the term skill must be redefined, and that the skills to be taught to future workers are of a different nature altogether than those needed in the past.

General Outcomes of Vocational Education

One reason why some critics of occupational education have been dissatisfied with the present program is their belief that, if permitted to do so, it could make a much greater contribution to the general development of many students. There have been frequent suggestions that vocational education, with its strong emphasis upon the doing types of activities, could offer an alternative path to learning for those with a low aptitude for verbal learning. The value of occupational education as a teaching-learning method may be greater for some students than its substantive value as skill training. The 1968 report of the Advisory Council on Vocational Education, strongly recommends this, especially in view of studies which have already been referred to which show that a relatively low proportion of high school students make occupational use of specific vocational skills learned in school.

The lack of evidence that occupational education can often re-motivate the student who is disinterested and alienated from school was discussed in Chapter 3, but this does not mean that vocationally oriented learning activities cannot be used as vehicles by many students for achieving general learnings. When combined with well coordinated work experiences in actual employment—experiences which are carefully related to in-school studies—the general education outcomes for the student can often be excellent. This is quite different from using vocational education strictly for job training and placement, and for this reason some vocational educators hesitate to accept it as legitimate form of occupational education. Nevertheless, under a broadened concept of occupational education it could well be included and further developed.

There are few vocational subjects that cannot be taught in a generalized fashion.[16] Just as students in their academic learnings need to do much more than store up facts and repeat them, so vocational students need to do more than acquire a repertoire of skills for doing particular jobs. Instead, their preparation should stress the ability to analyze, to assess, to compare, to weigh evidence, to decide—in short to think, and these abilities are as useful and necessary in vocational life as in other human activity.[17] They can be learned in a vocational setting as well as any other, and there is no reason why occupational education cannot make as great a contribution to this kind of general education as the so-called academic subjects are expected to do, for intellect, culture and vocation are inseparable.

Occupational Outcomes of General Education

What has already been said in this and previous chapters should be sufficient to establish the indispensable role of general education in the occupational success of the modern worker. No longer can a general liberal education be considered an adornment or a luxury designed primarily for the professional and leadership class, while the work of the world is done by skilled but rough hewn craftsmen with limited education. That era is long behind us, but some of the heritage it left still occurs at times in educational thinking. Former U. S. Commissioner of Education Francis Keppel has stressed the importance of basic academic studies for all students, whether college bound or not.[18] The fact is that the student who neglects his general education in favor of other vocational learning is being educationally cheated. In today's world a well rounded general education is not only a vocational asset for every young person, it is actually a functional requirement for maintaining himself in almost any kind of employment. The most needed change in occupational education is to recognize this and provide for it.

Are Vocational and General Education Separate Disciplines?

Despite many attempts to separate vocational education and general education in their organization, administration and curriculum planning, there have always been serious reservations about such arrangements on the part of many educators. These reservations have now reached the point where the most thoughtful and influential educational spokesmen, both vocational and general, agree that vocational and general education are not only compatible but that they are mutually supportive.[19] This has led the authors of the report, *The Bridge Between Man and His Work*, to say that "vocational education is not a separate discipline within education, but it is a basic objective of all education, and must be a basic element of each person's education."[20] If this conclusion is correct then a good many practices of the past will have to be altered and many of the fears, prejudices and animosities that have weakened the coordination of the two areas will have to be forgotten. With the present renewal of interest in occupational education and the national expectations for its larger role in American education, the time has come for this to happen. Certainly every step which will make it possible should be encouraged, and every attitude and action which stands in its way should be put aside.

Combining General and Occupational Education

The best way to combine the general with the vocational in education is to merge them in all educational planning and then treat education as a unitary process wherever it is carried on. It is not enough that the objectives of occupational education be agreed upon by the specialists in this field. They must be arrived at with the involvement of all who determine educational policy and practice. In other words, educational planning must become a joint enterprise which is shared in by both vocational and general educators in which both are willing to forfeit their identity and approach the education of the young as a common social need to be met.

The particular changes and arrangements to which this would lead need not be spelled out here. Most of the viewpoints and practices which tend to prevent the merging of occupational and general education are discussed in other chapters and in relation to other issues. Perhaps most important is to so organize the educational system so that no student is ever compelled to make a choice between his general education and his vocational preparation, and in choosing one, have to reject the other.

Summary

Whether education should serve liberal or practical ends has been a matter of philosophical controversy for centuries, and only a few have understood that it can and must do both. The conditions under which occupational education has developed in the United States have given it a strong utilitarian bias but this must now be adapted to meet the changing nature of occupations in a technological world. Vocational success in our society now depends fully as much upon general educational development as upon any specialized vocational skills, and to differentiate between the two becomes increasingly futile.

Occupational education has directed much of its effort toward preparation for initial job entry and his therefore tried to anticipate in its curriculums the special skills which employers will wish to buy. The evidence is that few employers are as much interested in these kinds of skills as they are in the more generalized qualifications of the applicant. Schools will serve youth best if they concentrate upon preparing them for a career rather than an entry job, and if they form partnerships with those who have jobs to offer, in order to help every student make a better transition from school to work.

Occupational education needs very much to widen its concept of what its goals should be, and to achieve a better balance between breadth and specialization. Such specialization as there is should come as late as possible in the educational process, and much of it will necessarily have to be learned on the job.

The theory that an individual's life consists of compartments corresponding to his different life roles and that he can be prepared for his role as a worker by a separate, special kind of education is unsound. Technology has made it impossible to separate technical from general learnings, and therefore made meaningless the age old distinction between culture and vocation, between the liberal and the practical, between general and vocational education. The two must now be joined in a single, unified kind of education for everyone and both general and vocational educators must combine their forces to this end.

REFERENCES

1. Whitehead, A. N. *The Aims of Education.* New York: Macmillan Co., 1964.
2. Brookover and Nosow. *Education for a Changing World of Work.*
3. Eninger. *The Process and Product of T and I Vocational Education in the United States.*
4. Kaufman and Schaefer. *The Role of the Secondary School in Preparing Youth for Employment.*
5. See Chapter 7.
6. Eninger. *The Process and Product of T and I Vocational Education in the United States.*
7. Ibid.
8. See Chapter 4.
9. National Advisory Council on Vocational Education. *First Annual Report.* Washington, D. C., 1969.
10. Venn. *Man, Education and Work.*
11. Kaufman and Schaefer. *The Role of the Secondary School in Preparing Youth for Employment.*
12. Russell, James E. *Change and Challenge in American Education.* Boston: Houghton Mifflin Co., 1965.

13. Great Cities School Improvement Council. *Report of the Western Regional Conference on Vocational Education*. Chicago: The Research Council of the Great Cities Program for School Improvement, 1967.
14. Advisory Council on Vocational Education. *Vocational Education: The Bridge Between Man and His Work*.
15. Ibid.
16. Provincial Committee on Aims and Objectives of Education in the Schools of Ontario. *Living and Learning*.
17. Russell. *Change and Challenge in American Education*.
18. Gordon, Margaret S., ed., *Poverty in America*. Proceedings of a National Conference held at the University of California at Berkeley, 1965. San Francisco: Chandler Publishing Comany, 1965.
19. Coppedge, Walter Raleigh. "DE's Affair with the Humanities." *American Vocational Journal* 45, no. 6 (September, 1970) : 70 ff.
20. Advisory Council on Vocational Education. *Vocational Education: The Bridge Between Man and His Work*.

CHAPTER 6

VOCATIONAL EDUCATION IN THE HIGH SCHOOL AND POST HIGH SCHOOL

Federally assisted vocational education in America has been conducted primarily for students in the public high schools, and in earlier days for students who had not completed an eighth grade education. At one time there were sound reasons for this because the great majority of young people moved into the labor market in their early teens, most of them without a high school education, and readily found a place there. Indeed, their earnings were needed by most working-class families. Today conditions are vastly different, but vocational education in the schools adjusts slowly and with reluctance to the change. Educators have been forced to recognize the growing trend toward deferring specialized training to the period beyond the high school and the two-year post secondary schools have, for the first time, been made eligible for federal funding by recent vocational education legislation. Yet the argument is still made that because many young people do not continue their formal education beyond the high school they must receive vocational training while they are still in school or they will be seriously handicapped in finding and keeping employment.

Several states now achieve high school graduation for eighty-five percent of their youth, and others will surely accomplish this in the future. Yet it is true that approximately twenty percent of non-urban youth still fail to complete high school, and this increases to thirty percent in large cities. The suggestion is frequently made that all of these students, in addition to all who do not enter college, should have acquired marketable skills, each for some particular occupation, before leaving high school. This theory has a number of flaws and one of them is the impossibility of knowing in advance who the dropout or the non-college student will be. Moreover, at least one major study has found that vocational courses taken in high school by students who later dropped out had no significant effect upon lowering their unemployment rates.[1] The study of Trade and Industrial graduates conducted by Eninger seems to confirm this by its finding that even for vocational graduates the advantages of their training, as compared with academic graduates, did not appear unless they were placed in the specific jobs for which they were trained.[2]

The need for those who complete high school to receive vocational training before they graduate because they may terminate their education at that point is no longer as important as it once may have been, for there has developed in the United States what amounts to a national policy to provide a minimum of fourteen years of public education for all, with the final two years, beyond the high school, devoted to occupational education for those who desire it. Many states have already accepted this goal and it will soon become public policy for the others. This national commitment was given authoritative expression by the National Commission of Technology, Automation and Economic Progress in its report, which recommended fourteen years of education for all and then went on to say, "For most secondary school pupils, vocational training should be deferred until after high school. The high school should emphasize broad general education in language and literature, mathematics and science, history and social studies and the arts. These subjects are an essential foundation not only for personal development and citizenship, but also for most vocations."[3]

The authorization for public funds to be spent for post secondary occupational education, which first appeared in the Vocational Education Act of 1963[4] and which was strengthened in the 1968 Vocational Education Amendment Act,[5] in effect establishes the place of vocational education beyond the high school as a desirable goal. Repeatedly, studies relating to the question of when occupational education should be offered recommend that vocational specialization be postponed until the student completes high school. The report of the Summer

Study of Occupational, Vocational and Technical Education held at the Massachusetts Institute of Technology contained such a recommendation. Ginzberg, an authority on economics and education, writing on the meaning of present-day social and economic trends makes the same proposal.[6] The report of the curriculum study made by the Ontario Department of Education reaches this same conclusion and most other evidence supports it.[7]

The Changing Age of Entrance Into the World of Work

The average age at which the labor market is ready to accept young workers is slowly but steadily rising. This means that young people can wait until they are older to receive vocational training (as opposed to occupational orientation and guidance), that they are, in fact, compelled to do so, and that, everything considered, it is more advantageous for them. It has long been axiomatic in vocational education that the more closely the actual training precedes its application on the job the more effective it becomes. For a number of reasons, all related to technology, the opportunity to enter employment for the first time is being progressively deferred in our society, and this should lead to a corresponding postponement of specialized occupational education in the school program.

There are several causes for this steady rise in the age of first job availability. One is the successful stay-in-school campaign conducted in recent years by government, business, education, industry and labor. This may, however, be a secondary cause, and a response to more fundamental influences. Nevertheless, it has convinced many American parents and their children of the value of an extended education. It has been repeatedly emphasized, by every medium of communication, that a good job requires a good education, and a good education has been equated with a longer education. The large increments in lifetime earnings which appear to result from each additional year of education have been frequently cited as an inducement for the young to seek more education. A stigma of failure has been attached by society for dropping out of school. Going to college has become a serious goal for all but the very poor and disadvantaged, and even for many of them.

The affluence which our society enjoys has, of course, added to the ability and therefore the desire of American families to keep their children in school longer. Local, state and national political leaders have responded to this by pouring more and more funds into more and more years of education for the nation's youth. They are well justified in doing so, for the needs of a modern society demand more and better education for its citizens.

Another reason for extending the period of schooling for youth may be that it is an indirect effort to cope with an otherwise troublesome effect of technology. The logic of technology and its handmaiden, automation, is that it can get more work done with fewer people at work. This could result in considerable technological unemployment, and society must find ways to meet this problem. One way is to discharge workers and tolerate higher unemployment, but this is unacceptable politically. Another is to so increase consumption that all who wish to work will be employed, but there are limits to this method of reducing the number of excess workers. Still another answer is the early retirement of older workers, and this policy is being widely adopted. Reduction in annual hours of work through more paid holidays and longer paid vacations is another device for absorbing more people into the work force who might otherwise be unemployed. Overall there has developed a strong social concensus against discharging an established worker even though technology may have made his services unnecessary, and this is increasingly supported by seniority and tenure provisions for union and government workers and by other social sanctions.

However, there are two other devices which are acceptable, and even approved, for dealing with the problem of excess manpower. One is known as "silent firing," which means that normal attrition is relied upon to reduce the number of workers needed or to greatly limit the number of replacements which would otherwise be required.[8] The other is to remove young people from the labor market by keeping them in school. The net result of both these policies is to raise the age of first employment, slowly but steadily, and we have now reached the point where little meaningful employment is available to those under twenty years of age.[9] This represents a probable increase of four to five years within one generation in the average age at which young people can permanently enter the world of work.

Every indicator and every technological influence points to a rising age of entrance into vocational life and more years of schooling for the average worker. This makes it not only possible but desirable to delay explicit occupational preparation longer and creates the need for a thorough reassessment of the traditional kinds of vocational education as a part of the high school curriculum.

High School and Post High School Enrollments

High school enrollments skyrocketed during the late nineteen fifties and the early sixties as a result of high postwar birth rates. These have now dropped and high school populations have accordingly stabilized, and for the foreseeable future they can only increase to the extent that the retention of students is improved. Thus whatever expansion of occupational enrollments may occur in the high school will not be caused by increases in the total student population. Yet if the program is redirected toward occupational orientation, career guidance, and generalized vocational preparation, and if it begins to serve the disadvantaged youth as it should, then every high school student can benefit from it, and its services at the high school level can expand enormously. This, rather than specialized training for specialized groups, is the approach that should be the future aim of vocational curriculum makers for high school youth.

In the post secondary field the situation is quite different. The two-year post secondary institutions represent the fastest growing segment of the American educational system, and there is every reason to believe that this growth has only begun. It will be further stimulated if the national defense policies now being initiated bring about the reductions in the armed forces that are now projected, leaving more young men free to pursue their education beyond high school. The principal causes of growth, however, are the lack of demand for teen-age youth in the labor market and the widespread public conviction that education beyond the high school has become essential for adequate employment and upward social mobility. The student population in higher education has doubled in the last fifteen years. A recent article in *Newsweek* magazine states that forty-five percent of college age youth now enrolls in higher education and that this may climb to seventy per-

cent during the next decade.[10] This figure is supported by
Russell who projects that sixty-eight percent of high school
graduates will be seeking further education during the same
period.[11]

Clearly the immediate post high school years now afford the
best and most appropriate time for young people to prepare
for their occupational specializations. This is what Barlow
means when he says that the future of vocational education
belongs to the post high school institution and that programs
involving segregation by occupational categories in the high
school will disappear in favor of a broader and more generalized curriculum.[12] This will compel not only the high schools,
but the two-year institutions beyond them to alter substantially their earlier roles in occupational education.

Consequences of Prolonged Education

In certain respects the constant lengthening of the period
of formal education can become a mixed blessing. Its effects
may not all be positive, either for society or for the individual.
Already our education extends the years of schooling for youth
far beyond that which any such group has previously enjoyed,
and well beyond what advanced contemporary nations now
attempt. If this is to continue, many traditional aims and forms
of American education, including those of occupational education, will have to be re-examined and probably greatly modified.

More years spent in school prior to embarking upon a vocational career postpones the opportunity for youth to enter
fully into adult life and to this extent creates an artificial
prolongation of childhood. American society places a premium
upon vocational success. One of its chief culture symbols of
achieving adulthood is to secure a job, earn an income, and no
longer be economically dependent upon parents or other adults.
When this is too long deferred many young people begin to
feel that they are marking time, they become frustrated and
impatient, and school and other social institutions become unattractive and, in their terms, irrelevant. It is possible that
the increasing number of years which must be spent in school
before being admitted to adult society may account for much
of the unrest and hostility which have so widely characterized
the students in our schools in recent years. There are many stu-

dents for whom it might be more valuable and more psychologically healthy if they could readily enter the world of work at the time when this becomes especially important to them, and this, of course, varies greatly with individuals. Yet so long as society frowns upon leaving school before completing a fixed block of education, and so long as schools at every level make it difficult to leave and re-enter their programs as need requires, this problem is likely to persist and perhaps intensify.

Unless significant changes are made in our educational and employment practices youth will continue to be caught in a cultural conflict which prizes work as a badge of responsible adulthood but makes them wait longer and longer for the opportunity to engage in it. The most successful programs of occupational education, by any measure, are those which combine actual work experience with in-school education, yet they are not widely found in practice. Distributive education is the only branch of occupational education that consistently makes use of this kind of program organization.[13] To extend this form of education to most students would require a much greater willingness than presently exists on the part of employers and labor groups to share in the occupational education of youth, and once again this brings about a conflict with older workers who wish to protect themselves from vocational competition with the young.

As the demand for more years of education continues, some very difficult and unpleasant social problems may result which will force us to reconsider our educational directions and the relation of our education to many other developments in American life.

Terminal vs Open-Ended Education

From the preceding discussion it should be abundantly evident that technology has brought educational demands which call for education beyond the high school for most of our future citizens and that the American public expects the educational system to provide it. Yet vocational education, throughout most of its history, has looked upon the high school as the terminal point in the educational process and has planned accordingly. It was with some reluctance that vocational educators accepted the change which came in 1963 and which permits federal funds to be used for occupational education in two-year and four-year colleges. Even now some vocational education spokesmen talk of the need to have eighty percent of high school youth receive vocational training geared to immediate entry into the labor market, whereas the figures and trends which have been cited would suggest quite the reverse.

As the high school passed through the era of serving as an advanced school for an elite minority and went on to become a people's college, enrolling everyone, so it has now emerged as terminal for a diminishing few. It therefore serves its students badly in their general as well as their vocational needs if it continues to think of itself as a school offering terminal education. In reality, no program of education at any level should any longer be planned as terminal, but all education in the future must be open-ended. This means a type of organizational and administrative flexibility which will permit an individual to depart from the program when his needs are met but also permit easy re-entry when desired and, most important, assure ready access to the next higher level of education and training.

The lack of an open-ended philosophy has been responsible for much of the stigma that has attached to occupational education because it has created the image of a dead-end form of education. Occupational education has been far too short-range in its objectives and too circumscribed in its goals, and it will never be well accepted by the American public until it overcomes these restrictions. No form of education can meet the needs of the next generation if it in any way hampers the further and continuing education of the individual.[14] To become open-ended, occupational education must be accepted as valid and intellectually respectable learning, and there is no reason why it cannot be made so.[15] The educational system has been understandably reluctant to consider as legitimate the kind of occupational education which is designed chiefly to provide a package of specialized job skills that can quickly become obsolete, but this need not and should not be characteristic of vocational education in the future. If education is to truly serve all our people so that, in the words of the motto of the State University of New York, "Each may become all that he is capable of becoming," all educational doors must be kept open and further education encouraged, until each individual approaches his capacity to absorb it.

Women in the Work Force

Although approximately half the women of working age in the United States are employed full time or part time, their need for occupational education has not been met by the programs in the schools. The exception to this has been in business education, in which most of the students are girls, but even here the emphasis has been narrow, mostly concentrated on typing and stenographic skills. The other offerings for women have been standard and stereotyped—namely cosmetology and occasionally some training in the garment trades. In the field of nursing the record is better, and girls dominate the registrations in distributive education courses. In all cases the program for girls has been tailored to fit the limited occupational categories which were specified in federal legislation prior to 1963, and to prepare for discrete kinds of jobs within those categories. Occupational education for women, as well as for men, has failed to provide a broad based and significant preparation for occupational life, although most women will spend some part of their lives as members of the labor force. If career orientation for boys has been inadequate, for girls it has been non-existent.

Vocational education has, instead, offered its major service to girls through the program of homemaking. It has long been recognized that the skills and arts of homemaking are not vocational in a wage earning sense, but that they are almost universally useful and essential, and that boys as well as girls can benefit by acquiring them. Therefore a very good argument can be made for including a broadly conceived form of homemaking education in the general life preparation of all youth. Under conditions of modern living the management of a home and family demands a more active sharing by both men and women than ever before and the wage earning careers of both may depend greatly upon their ability to do it successfully. However, homemaking is among the general areas of living and there appears to be no reason why it should be tied to occupational education.

A New Role for Occupational Education

In the light of what has been said, the question arises as to what role the high school and the schools beyond the high school should play in meeting the needs for occupational education during the years immediately ahead. There is no question that the need for it is greater than ever before and that the benefits of occupational education should be a part of the educational development of all youth, continuing to serve them as adults. But what kind of education should it be and what contributions should be expected from the various levels of schools and programs?

Probably the high school should withdraw altogether from the attempt to prepare any of its students for particular occupations. This would be done in recognition of the many reasons which make it relatively ineffective for most students at this age and period of vocational development and the lack of demand from the labor market for those who are so trained. These reasons are considered in the preceding discussion, and in other chapters. The high school, while not offering differentiated courses in vocational categories, would still make a strong contribution to future vocational success by cultivating general intellectual and social skills, personal qualities, and understandings of vocational life, all of which constitute a good deal of the fundamental preparation for being a worker. This could be done from a work related point of view, with a conscious goal by teachers and curriculum makers of preparing the student for his vocational life. In doing this, the high school should become pre-eminently the period during which career planning and decision making takes a top priority in the curriculum, for it is a time for vocational planning rather than vocational training. Vocational orientation, guidance, and exploration, much different and much more effective than that presently provided, should form a continuing part of every student's experience throughout the years of high school. The 1968 report of the Advisory Council on Vocational Education placed so much importance on this that it suggested that all the federal funds allocated to vocational education could be profitably spent for occupational orientation.[16]

Beyond the high school, occupational education should become more specialized, to the extent made necessary by developments in the world of work, and the career plans of the students. No magic change occurs when a student emerges from high school and enters a college, a community college, or some similar institution. He is only a few months older, and many of his general needs have not yet been satisfied.

Many such students have not yet made a clear vocational choice and will continue to need help in doing so. The two-year colleges are rapidly becoming the people's colleges which the high schools used to be, but a significant study in New York State by Knoell revealed the present weaknesses in high school guidance and counseling which are found in students of the two-year colleges of that state. It was found that entering students required a great deal of orientation with regard to their vocational goals and that this need contained throughout most of their two-year stay.[17] Hopefully, if there was a more effective program of career orientation in the lower schools, more students would be more advanced in their vocational planning and more certain of their career goals when they leave high school.

The two-year post secondary school, quite clearly, must be a multipurpose institution. For some students it can be a self testing experience as to their aptitude and motivation for further education through transfer into a four-year college or university. All who have had experience with students in two-year colleges are aware that many of them whose college potential was considered doubtful when they were in high school have, in the two-year program, demonstrated a very acceptable capacity for further collegiate work. Providing the opportunity for such students to thus find themselves has to be an accepted and respected goal of the two-year college. The opportunity to test and explore occupational interests must also be available. For a great many, perhaps most, students these schools will need to offer basic training leading to entrance into a wide variety of occupational areas, including many occupations that are now rejected by them as not being of collegiate caliber.

The forerunners of the emerging two-year colleges are to be found in two divergent kinds of institutions which appeared earlier upon the educational scene. One of these was the traditional junior college, which was wholly academic in character, often privately sponsored, and with a curriculum almost exclusively academic and liberal. The other was the two-year technical institute which existed in many parts of the country. These schools offered training in a limited number of engineering technologies, but few, if any liberal studies. The modern two-year or community college attempts to combine both kinds of programs in a comprehensive program, but it must do considerably more than this in order to render the educational service that it should. The occupational curriculums in present-day two-year colleges often started with some of the familiar technical courses related to engineering, and in many cases these still account for a large part of their registration. There has been a shortage of engineering technicians, although a study conducted by Pearce revealed that they comprise only two and one half percent of the work force in the highly industrialized state of New York, and that the need for them is rising very slowly.[18]

Recently the two-year colleges have been adding to the fields of occupational training available to their students, but in doing so they have tended to limit these fields to occupations which are closely related to the professions and which can be loosely classified as technical or para-professional. Few of these curriculums are planned for less than two years, and they usually culminate in an associate degree. This is done partly as a concession to academic respectability and partly to maintain the collegiate image. Many of these occupational curriculums are selective in their admission of students and this means that unless a student's high school record was quite good he cannot be accepted.

If the two-year colleges are to occupy the place they should in American education, and fulfill the purposes for which they are needed, some of these policies will have to be changed. Such schools will be required and should be ready to accept all high school graduates who apply, as those in California now do. They will need to add to their curriculum offerings in many occupations which are not of the para-professional type and which are more in the categories now found in the vocational courses of the high schools. Concern for the collegiate image and the emphasis upon the white collar occupations will have to be abandoned in favor of meeting the educational needs of all youth. Many of the occupations which should be introduced will not require two years of training and need not lead to a degree, but they must be offered on a full-time basis, side by side with the more technical and the degree programs. The first need of some students will be a period of remedial education together with intensive guidance and counseling so that they may discover their actual potential and formulate their goals.[19]

There seems to be no reason except that of academic prestige which would prevent the two-year colleges from accepting such multipurpose responsibilities. If they do not, then inevitably still another set of post secondary institutions will be created to do so, and the area vocational schools now being developed could well become the schools to fill the gap. It would be unfortunate if this came about. It would only add unnecessarily to the fragmentation of the educational system, and to its complexity, and would be another step toward educational separatism. It would also impose unnecessary construction, administrative and operational costs upon the public. A more sensible plan would be for the present area vocational schools to gradually become comprehensive and multipurpose post secondary schools.

Summary

Occupational education in the United States has been directed toward students in high school because until 1963 the federal funds which supported it could not be spent for courses of college grade. Although this is now permitted and encouraged, vocational educators continue to think and plan largely in terms of the high school student.

In sharp contrast to earlier periods, the majority of high school graduates now move on to some form of further education. At the same time there are a number of developments which tend to close the labor market to teen-age youth, and the typical age for entry into full-time employment continues to rise. High school can no longer be thought of as terminal education for anyone and therefore the need for specialized vocational training is disappearing from the high school and is becoming the responsibility of the next higher level of education.

The extension of education beyond the high school for many young people may be in part a response to a need to limit the competition with older workers by the young, and can help to prevent some technological unemployment. It also fits very well into the need for more education for most jobs in today's economy. Although all of the effects of prolonged schooling are not favorable, either for the individual or for society, there appears to be no possibility that the trend will be reversed.

Occupational education has not given to women as workers the attention which is commensurate with their prominent role in today's labor force. It should review and update its programs for girls and women, and should treat the subject of homemaking as general education for both boys and girls. The weight of evidence favors the withdrawal of the high school from programs of training for specific categories of occupations and the postponement of occupational specialization to the post secondary period. In its place the high school should develop a truly functional program of occupational orientation, career planning and decision making. The two-year post high school institutions must then serve as universal staging areas for either further education or entry into the labor market, in addition to accepting a number of related but important responsibilities. To do this they will have to disregard their preoccupation with maintaining a quasi-collegiate status, and subordinate academic prestige to the broader welfare of their students.

REFERENCES

1. Perrella, V., and Bogan, F. "Out of School Youth." Special Labor Force Report no. 46, part 1. *United States Department of Labor Review* (November, 1964).
2. Eninger. *The Process and Product of T and I Vocational Education in the United States.*
3. National Commission on Technology, Automation, and Economic Progress. *Technology and the American Economy*, vol. 1. Washington, D. C.: U. S. Government Printing Office (February, 1966).
4. U. S. Congress. *Vocational Education Act of 1963*. Public Law 88-210, 88th Cong., 1963.
5. U. S. Congress. *Vocational Education Amendments Act, 1968*.
6. Barlow. *Vocational Education.*
7. Provincial Committee on Aims and Objectives of Education in the Schools of Ontario. *Living and Learning.*
8. Blum, Albert. "Automation, Education and Unemployment." *Phi Delta Kappan* 51, no. 10 (June, 1970): 555-557.
9. Advisory Council on Vocational Education. *Vocational Education: The Bridge Between Man and His Work.*
10. Article on Education. *Newsweek.* June 15, 1970.
11. Russell. *Change and Challenge in American Education.*
12. Barlow. *Vocational Education.*
13. Advisory Council on Vocational Education. *Vocational Education: The Bridge Between Man and His Work.*
14. Gardner, John. *Excellence: Can We Be Equal and Excellent Too?* New York: Harper and Row, Publishers, 1961.
15. Venn. *Man, Education and Work.*
16. Advisory Council on Vocational Education. *Vocational Education: The Bridge Between Man and His Work.*

17. Knoell, Dorothy M. *Toward Educational Opportunities for All.* Report of a study of the Community and other two year colleges in New York State. Albany: The State University of New York, 1966.
18. New York State Department of Labor, Division of Research. *Technical Manpower in New York State.* Albany: N. Y. State Dept. of Labor (December, 1964).
19. Knoell. *Toward Educational Opportunities for All.*

CHAPTER 7

VOCATIONAL EDUCATION
AND RESEARCH

The History of Vocational Education Research

The Smith-Hughes law and subsequent federal legislation authorized the expenditure of funds for studies which might benefit vocational education, but not until the passage of the Vocational Education Act of 1963 were specified amounts of the federal appropriations earmarked and set aside solely for the purposes of research.[1,2] Good research is costly, and the amounts of money appropriated under Smith-Hughes were small, so that when they were distributed over the fifty states no state felt that it could spare money for research when it was so badly needed to operate their programs. Neither was the United States Office of Education in a position to finance any meaningful research from its limited vocational funds. Until quite recently the large private foundations, which frequently made grants for the study of education, especially higher education, showed no interest in supporting research in occupational education.

Prior to 1963, therefore, what little research there was in occupational education produced only minor studies and had to be carried on through the resources of professional organizations such as the American Vocational Association or of some university departments or by individuals preparing doctoral dissertations. None of these had adequate funds or personnel to make a significant research contribution, and coordination of effort, means for disseminating results and for field testing and demonstration were entirely lacking. In 1955 a group of educators representing the largest cities in the United States met with some of the national leaders in vocational education in an attempt to initiate studies which would lead to the improvement of occupational education in those cities. A small grant from the Sears-Roebuck Foundation was used to get these studies under way, and a good beginning was made. This developed into a permanent organization of these cities, now known as the Great Cities School Improvement Research Council, which later sponsored studies into numerous other educational problems of urban communities and its research efforts have made important contributions to this end.[3] Once again, however, its resources were limited and uncertain, and the continuing, depth research which was so much needed in occupational education could not be accomplished.

All of these shortcomings produced two weaknesses in the program of vocational education. One result was that it developed and continued to operate without benefit of the kinds and quality of research which were bringing improvement to many other areas of education and for which federal, university and foundation research funds were available. Policies and practices in occupational education were based many times upon armchair opinion and assumptions which were never subjected to research testing or critical review. The second result was that a generation of vocational educators grew up who had little contact with research and who were unprepared either to engage in it or to make use of its findings when the opportunity for worthwhile research finally came.

Largely as a result of recommendations made by the Panel of Consultants on Vocational Education, the Vocational Education Act of 1963 provided that ten percent of the funds appropriated should be spent for research in occupational education, to be shared by the United States Office of Education and the individual states.[4] This placed at the disposal of researchers the needed resources on a scale vastly greater than had ever before been available. Actually they were not prepard to use such amounts of money quickly and usefully, but plans and preparations were made, and since that time, although research funding has flutuated from year to year, there has been much progress and an astonishing amount of research has been produced.

In addition to federal research money some private foundations, notably the Ford Foundation, have awarded substantial grants for research in vocational education. This foundation has also sponsored a number of conferences on vocational education for discussions of studies and research and has also established a center for studies in occupational education at the University of Wisconsin. It has also added to its staff a program officer in vocational education.

The evidence of new interest and activity in vocational education research is widespread. Two major centers for research in this field have been established with federal support, one at Ohio State University and another at the University of North Carolina. Ohio State has also become the Educational Research Information Center (ERIC) for the collection, computer storage and retrieval of all aspects of research relating to occupational education, a service having much value to research workers. A research and development branch in occupational education has been established in the United States Office of Education. Beyond this, every state has created a research coordinating unit for occupational education within its State Education Department. These state coordinating agencies and the United States Office of Education have distributed large amounts of research money in the form of grants to universities and other research organizations for a wide variety of research projects. In 1970 the Congress appropriated more than $350,000,000 for grants to the states for vocational education, and the states were required to spend ten percent of this money, or $35,000,000 for research. This was a tremendous advance in funding for a program which only seven years ago received no funds whatever, and persons with research interests and skills have responded with a growing output of research in occupational education and related fields. In 1965 a small group of vocational educators met informally to discuss the formation of an association to promote and disseminate vocational education research. In the short period since that time this has become the large and flourishing American Vocational Education Research Association and an active division of the American Vocational Association.

Within the space of a few years, then, research activities in occupational education have grown from a few feeble, poorly supported projects by a few individuals into a well financed, vigorous program involving many people and resources. The time is here when it is fair to ask what the fruits of this research have been, what positive effects have resulted for vocational education and what may be expected in the future. At this point the answers to some of these questions would not be very encouraging, for it would be difficult to find many significant changes or improvements in operating programs which have resulted from the research which has been done. Perhaps there have been too few demonstration projects, too little field testing, or inadequate provision for disseminating the findings. Perhaps a movement which has relied so little upon research for so long has not yet learned to profit from it. Some mistakes have been made and perhaps the proper priorities have not always been set, but it is certainly true that for the first time occupational education research has received the recognition and support which it needs to make a major contribution to program improvement. The question which remains is whether it will be allowed to have an impact upon program goals and operations.

The Potential of Occupational Education Research

The potential of research for producing a better program of occupational education is very great. Few of the time honored beliefs and practices with which the movement has grown up have been research tested. They have been assumed, and the assumptions have gradually taken on the character of wisdom and truth, then adopted as policy through legislation. At this point they are no longer subject to question. Brandon and Evans have suggested a few of these assumptions. Among them are the assumed need for long occupational experience by vocational teachers and leaders, the assumed need for large blocks of time for learners to perfect vocational skills, the assumption that skills learned in school function later in jobs, and others.[5] Most of the traditional policies usually favored by vocationalists relating to organization, administration, curriculum development, career planning, finance, and teacher qualifications need to be validated or rejected through the application of rigorous research. Good research can dispel educational myths and open the door for new and better ways of doing things, but it cannot do so unless its findings are accepted and used.

One of the long-standing attitudes that has persisted among vocational educators is a strong prejudice against permitting persons who have been trained in industrial arts to teach vocational courses or to administer vocational programs. These policies have been defended on the grounds that such persons lack sufficient experience as a worker in industry and this has been held to be essential for success as a teacher or administrator. Yet there have been many cases where no fully qualified vocational candidate was available and where an industrial arts graduate has been employed for the job, and most of them have been very successful. In not a few cases they have later become outstanding leaders in the vocational education movement, yet the conventional wisdom maintains that they are not qualified for the task. Some well designed research could long ago have shown whether there was any merit in the arguments which have been raised on both sides of this question.

Another belief which has prevailed for years, and which has been referred to earlier, is that vocational education has been given a bad image by social prejudice and by unfriendly or biased school administrators and guidance counselors.[6] Instead of continuing to repeat these untested assumptions, research should be employed to throw some light upon the subject and perhaps put to rest what may be an educational myth. On the other hand, if such prejudice can be actually shown to exist its causes might be pinpointed so that efforts to combat it could be planned more effectively.

These are but a few of a long list of problems confronting occupational education which could be dealt with more rationally with the help of appropriate research. Research has led to spectacular breakthroughs in our hardware technology, in health care, in agriculture and in other facets of American life and there is no reason why it cannot serve education as well. In occupational education the list of problems in need of research is so long that priorities will have to be assigned so that the funds and personnel which are available may be used to the best advantage. For although present funding seems generous when compared to the meager support of the past, it is still relatively small for a segment of American education with so large an accumulated backlog of research needs. During deliberations of the House-Senate Conference Committee on the 1970 appropriations for vocational education, Congressman Roman Pucinski stated that only through research can the vocational education needs of the country be properly understood.[7]

Research in Related Areas

Many vocational educators have not yet recognized that research in other branches of education and in several of the disciplines other than education can be of great value to those guiding the direction of occupational education. Some of these have had a much longer history of research activity than vocational education can claim and they have developed extensive research literatures. In these fields, too, research is on the increase, and useful findings which can benefit occupational education continue to flow.

Past and recent research in guidance, counseling and career development, for example, is not only related to occupational education, it is actually locked in with its program, and all vocational educators should be familiar with it. The same can be said for research in manpower economics and for a wide range of other manpower problems. A great many studies have been carried out on these topics by departments of federal and state government, by schools of Business Administration and schools of Labor Relations in universities. Vocational educators should have knowledge of what these kinds of studies have to say about preparation for employment. Research in learning theory, of which there is a great deal, is surely as vital to the problems of vocational educators as it is to those who work in general education. The same can be said for research in curriculum and curriculum theory, in educational administration, in instruction and in finance. Vocational educators should be as well informed as any other modern educator about what research is reporting about these matters.

Research in program evaluation is taking on a new importance. There is at present a strong trend toward imposing a greater degree of accountability upon public education at all levels, which requires educators to justify their practices and to account for their results more than ever before. This kind of evaluation therefore becomes a major responsibility of those who conduct educational affairs. The recent vocational legislation calls for periodic, rather frequent evaluation of all vocational programs, state by state, and for evidence that necessary changes take place when such evaluation suggests the need for them. This means that research into better ways for evaluating vocational education will be badly needed, for this has been one of its weakest features.

An area that has been researched extensively in recent years is the education of the disadvantaged, and vocational educators should surely become acquainted with the principal findings of this research. They are required, under the new legislation, to devote significant amounts of their resources to the service of those who are classified as disadvantaged. Another subject which has been extensively researched is the sociology of occupations, but few vocational educators are familiar with it. The research literature in this field can help those who plan programs of occupational education and it should engage their interest and become a part of their professional knowledge.

Research Prior to 1960

It must be already evident that before the enactment of the Vocational Education Act of 1963, research in occupational education, while not completely neglected, was sparse, spasmodic, and often superficial. The reasons for this have already been discussed. Findings of this research were frequently based upon inadequate samplings.[8, 9] It was not possible to apply the best of research techniques to many of the problems in occupational education because to do so required a level of financing which was not then available. This is why the new resources supplied by recent legislation have been so welcome and so quickly accepted by those interested in improving occupational education through research. The effect should be that vocational education should in the future be influenced much more by research findings than it was during the first fifty years of its history.

Research Since 1960

The 1962 report of the Panel of Consultants on Vocational Education stimulated not only some milestone legislation but also an outpouring of new literature in the field of occupational education. Much of this has not taken the form of formal, designed research but rather the form of expository writing, representing the views of well qualified scholars and writers. This by no means detracts from its value. As already noted, there has also been a great amount of true research—so much, in fact, that it is well beyond the scope and purpose of this book to attempt a comprehensive review of it.

A great many of the writings and a number of the researches have already been referred to and others will be cited in later chapters. However, a few of the more significant studies which have been completed since 1960 will be briefly described in order to illustrate the range and diversity of the research of the recent past. These include official studies and surveys by commissions, councils and similar bodies, and studies conducted by individual investigators and teams of researchers.

Following the report of the 1962 Panel, the report of the 1967 Advisory Council on Vocational Education, entitled *Vocational Education: The Bridge Between Man and His Work*, was the next attempt to evaluate the program nationally. Both studies were comprehensive, insightful, candid and positive. Both reports pinpointed and documented program weaknesses and made recommendations for improvement. The studies by Eninger[10] and others by Kaufman,[11] Frank,[12] Coleman,[13] Burt,[14] Draper,[15] and Kemp[16] all brought fresh insights to questions which in some cases have been matters of debate for many years. Some of the findings confirmed the shortcomings which the critics of vocational education had often pointed out, while in other respects the program appeared favorably.

Our understanding of manpower problems and their relation to education was increased considerably by such reports as that of the National Commission on Automation, Technology and the American Economy,[17] the study by Arnstein for the National Education Association,[18] Rosenberg's study on Automation and Education[19] and those sponsored by the Upjohn Institute,[20] as well as numerous others. The annual Manpower Reports of the President have proved to be of great value for vocational educators.[21]

A great deal of research was generated during the 1960s relating to career development and occupational choice. Much of it was directed toward the formulation of theories of occupational behavior that would better explain these processes and avoid the weaknesses of the older trait-factor approach which have been described in Chapter 3. Researches by Crites, Lohnes, Tiedeman, Cooley, Super, Havighurst and Flanagan have led to better understandings of the dynamics of vocational choice and have raised some serious questions about some of the traditional practices of vocational education.[22]

Research in curriculum development has been on the increase during the past decade, and some new and promising theories are emerging. Many of the curriculum innovations which have been tried in general education are transferable to occupational education and some researchers have been working in this direction. Programmed instruction, computer assisted instruction, flexible scheduling, team teaching, multi-media learning, and curriculum evaluation can and should be applied to occupational education. A number of studies have dealt with the special problems of the occupational education curriculum. The possibilities of constructing the curriculum around families or clusters of occupations and thus reducing the disadvantage of overspecialization in the vocational curriculum have been investigated by Allen, Altman, and Maley among others.[23]

Few, if any, well designed studies have yet been made to probe unanswered questions relating to the organization and administration of occupational education. Most of what has been done has been descriptive and empirical in character and has done little to produce innovation in the ways in which vocational education is structured or controlled. In occupational education, patterns of organization and administration remain rooted in traditions, which were established in the early federal legislation and its administrative codes, and which have seen little significant change since that time. This is an area that needs a great deal of searching investigation and experiment. Some useful studies have been made by Lee, Levitan, Smith and McLure, but, generally speaking, only a small beginning has been made.[24] Advances in other aspects of occupational education depend to a large extent upon finding more flexible and tradition-free ways to provide for its organization and its administration. It has suffered seriously from the tendency to have its programs administered through legislation.

Evaluating the results of educational programs has always presented difficulties because it involves the measurement of human behavior—a task which is never easy or precise. Occupational education has lacked many of the testing and evaluative devices applied in other branches of education, and it is especially in need of research for such purposes. There is under way presently a national assessment program for education as a whole, but it has been the subject of much controversy and it is making very slow progress. Occupational education is included in its planning, with the hope of discovering ways to assess the outcome of its program, but there is much work to be done before this can be accomplished.

Some valuable work on program evaluation has been done, but much more is needed. Follow-up studies of vocational graduates on a scale broad enough to warrant some generalizations have been reported by Flanagan, Eninger and by Kaufman and his associates. Some cost-benefit analyses which attempt to relate the cost of occupational education to its measureable economic benefits have been conducted by a few investigators, again including Kaufman. As yet, however, occupational education is seriously lacking in the means for assessing the extent to which it is meeting its goals.

Although there has clearly been a great and welcome increase in research activity in occupational education during the decade of the 1960s, the quantity is still small when compared with the research to be found in such fields as reading, learning theory, or general theories of administration, to mention only a few examples. Also, good research usually raises new questions to be further researched, which is just beginning to happen in the case of occupational education. Still, if the commitment to research is maintained there is every reason to believe that it will bring benefits to vocational education which have long been denied it.

Personnel For Research in Occupational Education

The lack of encouragement and opportunity for doing research in occupational education over a long period of time resulted in a serious lack of qualified researchers within the movement itself. There were always a few who were both interested and qualified, and these few were chiefly responsible for whatever research was done. Yet when the resources for a greatly expanded research program finally became available the shortage of trained personnel quickly appeared. Fortunately, well trained researchers from other fields displayed an interest in occupational education research and although many of them had no background in vocational education they often teamed up with vocational specialists and many of them have made excellent contributions through their work.

In addition to the lack of trained research talent within their own ranks, vocational practitioners often lacked an understanding of the nature and requirements of research, and this has somewhat nullified the benefits of the research which has been done. Many practitioners have tended to be skeptical of research and to have little faith in its findings unless (a) it is done by a bona fide vocationalist and (b) the findings agree with existing beliefs and practices. It may require a new generation of vocational leaders who understand and respect research and who know how to use it before it can become fully effective.

It has been difficult for some vocational educators to understand that the particular background of a researcher is irrelevant so long as his research training is good and his research skills are sound. They also fail to understand that neither the researcher nor the research are concerned with what the findings may be or whether they support or conflict with present beliefs or practices, but only that they be scientifically defensible. They cannot be rejected because they are incompatible with the biases of anyone. These more objective attitudes toward research will in all likelihood become better established with better training of vocational educators—a training which will expose them to the nature, purposes and techniques of research. It may also be hoped that the new programs for preparing vocational leaders which are being initiated under the provisions of the Vocational Education Amendments Act of 1968 will produce a number of people who will specialize in research in their own field.

The Vocational Leader and Research

The reason why research in the physical sciences and the life sciences has revolutionized life in the modern world is the eagerness and speed with which new discoveries are accepted and exploited if they offer any promise of better living. Better ways for producing goods and food and for improving health are actively sought out through research and when benefits are demonstrated they are quickly and widely adopted. The same cannot be said for education, for here the results of research are slow to be recognized and slower still to be accepted. This is a special problem in occupational education. As the growing contributions of research in this field are produced they will have little effect unless those who operate programs accept and use the findings. A positive attitude toward research, and a desire to profit from it, even when cherished beliefs are challenged, must be found among those in positions of leadership in vocational education. They must be as willing to embrace change in their field as the medical profession is, in the light of tested new knowledge, to revise its methods for treating disease.

The vocational teacher and administrator of the future must relate to research in at least two important ways. He must become a knowledgeable consumer of research and he must, at times, become a participant in research. As a research consumer he must know how to keep himself informed of the research that is being done and he must also be capable of reviewing it critically so that he can judge its quality and its relevance to his own needs. Research requires adequate data which frequently can come only from the study of present programs, their students and graduates, personnel and curriculums, and the cooperation and help of administrators and teachers are often necessary for the success of such research projects. Here again, enough knowledge of research is needed to be able to evaluate the potential of a proposed project and to decide whether it is worthy of such support. Most of all there is need for the practitioners to look upon research as a continuing and indispensable resource for improving their programs.[25]

Summary

The use of quality research as a tool for improving knowledge and practice has been late in coming to the field of occupational education. This was caused largely by an early lack of resources but this lack has been recently and rapidly overcome by substantial appropriations of federal and state funds and by legal and official encouragement for research. Yet during its long period of development prior to 1960 almost every concept and policy in occupational education resulted from untested opinions and assumptions, or, at times, political necessity.

The potential for program improvement through research in occupational education is as great as in any other area of education, and probably greater because of the accumulated needs which have only now begun to be met. Nearly every aspect of vocational education needs to be critically examined and, through research, either validated or changed, and this must be a continuing process.

The 1962 report of the Panel of Consultants and the Vocational Education Act of 1963 brought a renewal of interest and an urgent emphasis to vocational education research and provided the means for supporting it. In contrast to the meager production of such research before that time, the past decade has seen a large amount of useful research, and a recognition that research in many related fields is germane to the problems of occupational education. Many well qualified researchers not formerly identified with vocational education have come forward to conduct studies and they have made a fine contribution to its research literature.

The fact that those doing the research in many cases have had little previous experience in occupational education has caused some vocational educators to be skeptical of the findings of their research. This is an attitude that must be overcome if vocational education is to benefit as it should from the research being done. Its administrators and teachers need a better understanding of the nature and requirements of research and they need to be more objective in assessing its findings. They must recognize that a researcher without a vocational education background may be more detached, and therefore more objective, than someone with deep commitments to present practice. On the other hand it is important that more vocational educators than in the past should make research their major professional interest and actively engage in it. It is also important that the professional preparation of all vocational education leaders and teachers includes a thorough grounding in the basic principles of research.

One of the weakest parts of the research program in occupational education has been the limited extent to which the results have been brought to the attention of the planners and practitioners. This weakness has been recognized but as yet no really satisfactory means for quick and wide dissemination of research findings has been found. As a result it is not uncommon to find vocational teachers, program directors and others who have not heard of some of the most significant research of the last few years, and this must be corrected or the research program will become limited to researchers talking to each other.

Future leaders of occupational education, as consumers of research, will have to know how to evaluate the quality of this research, determine its application to their problems, and be willing to be guided by its results.

REFERENCES

1. U. S. Congress. *Smith-Hughes Act.*
2. U. S. Congress. *Vocational Education Act of 1963.*
3. Great Cities School Improvement Research Council. *Research Reports.* Chicago: Research Council of the Great Cities for School Improvement, 1957-1967.
4. Brookover and Nosow. *Education for a Changing World of Work.*
5. Barlow. *Vocational Education.*
6. Workman, Glenn O. "Schoolmen Blamed for Image Problem." *American Vocational Journal* 45, no. 6 (September, 1970) : 8.
7. Schuchat, Theodore. "From Washington." *School Shop* 30, no. 1 (September, 1970) : 77.
8. Harris, Chester W., ed., *Encyclopedia of Educational Research*, 3rd Edition. Articles on Vocational Education and Trade and Industrial Education. New York: Macmillan Company, 1960.
9. Barlow. *Vocational Education.*
10. Eninger. *The Process and Product of T and I High School Level Vocational Education in the United States.*
11. Kaufman and Schaefer. *The Role of the Secondary School in Preparing Youth for Employment.*
12. Massachusetts Institute of Technology. *Report of the Summer Study on Occupational, Vocational and Technical Education.*
13. Coleman, James, and others. *Equality of Educational Opportunity.* Washington, D. C.: U. S. Government Printing Office, 1967.
14. Burt, Samuel M. *Industry and Technical Vocational Education.* New York: McGraw-Hill Co., 1967.
15. Draper, Dale C. *Educating for Work.* Washington, D. C.: National Association of Secondary School Principals, 1967.
16. Kemp, Barbara. *The Youth We Haven't Served.* U. S. Office of Education, OE-80038. Washington, D. C.: U. S. Government Printing Office.
17. National Commission on Technology, Automation, and Economic Progress. *Technology and the American Economy.*
18. Evans, Luther, and Arnstein, George. *Automation and the Challenge to Education.* Washington, D. C.: National Education Association, 1961.
19. Rosenberg, Jerry. *Automation, Manpower and Education.* New York: Random House, 1966.
20. Levitan, Sal. *Vocational Education and Federal Policy.* Kalamazoo, Michigan: Upjohn Institute of Employment Research, 1963.
21. U. S. Department of Labor. *Manpower Report of the President.* Washington, D. C.: U. S. Government Printing Office, annually since 1960.
22. American Educational Research Association. *Review of Educational Research Vocational, Technical and Practical Arts Education.* Washington, D. C.: American Educational Research Association (October, 1968).
23. Ibid.
24. Ibid.
25. Leighbody. *Organization and Operation of a Local Program of Vocational Education,* Chapter 13.

CHAPTER 8

OCCUPATIONAL EDUCATION AND THE DISADVANTAGED

The New Visibility of the Disadvantaged

As in any society, there has always existed in America a segment of the population which was at the lower end of the economic and social scale. This has been known to most Americans, and various kinds of public and private welfare measures have always been used to make the lot of these people as tolerable as possible. On the whole, however, they have been submerged and ignored by their fellow citizens and they have tended to endure, if not accept, their plight.[1]

With the great increase in general affluence which gradually came to the more fortunate majority after World War II, the economic and social disparity between this majority and those who shared least in the national benefits became so sharp as to be clearly evident to all. In addition, those at the bottom level found their conditions so intolerable that they became highly militant and vocal in their efforts to secure relief. This movement has been closely intertwined with the struggle for civil rights which has occurred during the same period. It has led to serious social disruptions, to a growing public awareness and a growing concern for the needs of the deprived, and to a search for ways to raise their economic and social status. The plight of the poor is now on the nation's conscience to a greater degree than ever before. It is now accepted in America that every citizen is entitled not only to his full civil rights but also to a job and to the basic comforts and personal dignity which come with a reasonable degree of economic security. The Employment Act of 1946 in effect sets this as a national goal.

The poor and the disadvantaged have now become highly visible and many efforts are being made to help them overcome their handicaps. Since jobs are the source of income, and since vocational education in its various forms is presumed to lead to jobs, it has been natural that public authorities should turn to it as a major weapon in the war on poverty.

Who Are The Disadvantaged?

The word disadvantaged has come into use to designate those who fall into the lowest economic and social level of our society. It is a euphemism for more accurate but less pleasant words which could be used to describe their condition. The basic and most universal characteristic of the people in this group is that they are poor, in many cases desperately poor. At times the government agencies which are set up to help them have attempted to set minimum incomes below which families or individuals would be officially labeled as disadvantaged and would be entitled to supplementary income from government sources. At one time an annual income of $3000 for a family of four was used as the cut off point for this purpose, and families whose income fell below this were designated as disadvantaged. This amount has been raised slightly from time to time. The federal legislation which has been proposed to reform the national welfare system uses a figure of a $1600 annual income, below which the income would be augmented by the government. Whatever the dollar amounts, they are still so low that they could only support subsistence living at best, and those receiving them would still be very low on the economic scale, with a large gap between them and the rest of the population. To be poor is to be disadvantaged, but the disadvantaged are impoverished in many other ways as well.

They live in the poorest housing, often unfit for habitation, being unable to afford any better. They exist on inadequate diets and often have insufficient food of any kind. They frequently lack proper sanitation and other health necessities and this, combined with their poor diets, results in chronic bad health for many of them, which in turn interferes with their ability to work steadily. Their lack of income forces them to occupy the crowded, deteriorating urban slums or to accept isolated rural slum living, and in the case of the American Indian, the reservation slum. What is of greatest concern to educators is the fact that they have the least and poorest education of any group in the population, and because of this and other deficiencies they suffer the largest amount of unemployment and underemployment. These rates are, for them, often many times the rate for other workers. All major racial groups in the nation can be found among the disadvantaged, but Black Americans, Spanish speaking Americans and American Indians predominate in the disadvantaged group. They constitute far larger percentages of the disadvantaged than they do in the general population, and whites constitute far less. This means that in addition to their other handicaps many of them suffer from racial and ethnic prejudice as well.[2]

It has already been noted that young people under the age of twenty and the poorly educated and unskilled of all ages face the most difficulty in getting jobs in our technological economy. Quite naturally, the disadvantaged individual is most affected by this problem, and the disadvantaged youth most of all. In 1965, while 11 percent of white youth were unemployed, this rose to 27 percent for nonwhite youth.[3] Since non-whites are much more likely to be disadvantaged, this would indicate that a disadvantaged youth is almost three times as vulnerable to unemployment as his more favored neighbor. The same kind of disparity is to be found among the adults of both groups. These kinds of statistics carried great weight with the Congress when it was drafting the Vocational Education Act of 1963, and again when revisions were made by passing the Vocational Education Amendments Act of 1968. During the debates on the latter legislation the Chairman of the House Subcommittee on Education stated that the very keystone to preparing people, particularly the disadvantaged, for jobs is vocational education, and that if earlier advantage had been taken of this program the problem of the hard core unemployed would not exist today.[4] Although this probably overstates the capacity of vocational education to solve the unemployment problems of the disadvantaged, a different kind of occupational education than that which has been available, and different attitudes toward the disadvantaged by vocational educators could no doubt have made a much greater contribution to their needs.

A study conducted in 1965 in a typical rural county of New York State showed that 92 percent of the disadvantaged students who had dropped out of school during the previous year had one or both parents who had also dropped out of school.[5] Unfortunately, the schools which serve the urban slums, and many rural schools, have been unprepared to meet the special needs of the disadvantaged and have served them poorly. Because a good education is essential for any kind of stable employment it seems logical that if children from disadvantaged environments could achieve such an education, the cycle of poverty, and therefore the other difficulties that arise from deprivation could be broken. It also seems logical to believe that if unemployment results from lack of skills, vocational education, by teaching skills, should make people employable. Actually the problem is not so easily solved. The skills required turn out to be the kind that vocational education has not usually taught, and even after much compensatory education has been offered the results in terms of educational achievement and employment have often been disappointing. There is evidence that racial and other forms of prejudice are still causing unemployment and especially underemployment among the disadvantaged groups, even after they have achieved educational equality, and that hiring practices and union restrictions often nullify the work of the job trainers. There is also evidence that vocational training has prepared the disadvantaged for low-skilled, dead-end jobs—jobs which may be eliminated soonest by technology.[6]

Can Vocational Education Eliminate Poverty?

Since the beginning of the latter-day concern with improving the condition of the poor great emphasis has been placed upon job training as a means for getting the unemployed quickly into jobs and for accomplishing the longer term objective of breaking the poverty cycle. Every piece of educational, vocational, manpower and welfare legislation which has been passed or proposed since 1960 has contained provisions for training. Government, at least, has pinned its hopes upon education, and particularly vocational education as the answer to the needs of the disadvantaged. The Manpower Development and Training Act of 1962[7], the Vocational Education Act of 1963[8], the Elementary and Secondary Education Act of 1965[9], The Economic Opportunity Act with its Job Corps[10], and the Vocational Education Amendments Act of 1968[11]—all have identified education and training as the principal weapon for fighting poverty and as the means for the salvation of the disadvantaged. The JOBS program for on-the-job training of the disadvantaged by private industry has concentrated on training as the major approach. The reform welfare legislation proposed by President Nixon in August of 1969 relies heavily upon job training to solve the problems of unemployment and poverty.

Yet serious doubts are beginning to appear as to the extent to which job training, as such, can alleviate the plight of the disadvantaged. None of the programs which have been tried have been more than marginally successful, and in order to produce the limited results that have been achieved it has been necessary to deal with a great many social and individual problems which had not always been anticipated. Furthermore, the long term value of this training is less apparent than many had hoped. It may help some individuals to meet their immediate needs, but it fails to reach the larger problems which form the roots from which poverty grows. The costs involved in getting an unemployed individual into regular employment have been very high, but however high the costs they are still less than the economic, personal and social price of lifetime unemployment.

What is discouraging is the failure of any of the programs yet tried to diminish the stream of unemployable disadvantaged youth which continues to pour into the labor market. The second report of the National Advisory Council on Vocational Education, issued in 1969, deplores this and stresses the futility of rehabilitating the unemployed if their ranks continue to be filled by those emerging from the schools.[12] The Council suggests that if only there was more vocational education in the schools, available to the disadvantaged, their future unemployment would be prevented. As most vocational education is now organized and conducted this is a dubious assumption.

There is every reason to believe that what prevents the disadvantaged from finding and maintaining employment is not lack of job training, but rather the absence of a sound and complete general education. It must be re-emphasized that the jobs in today's labor market cannot be performed without a substantial mastery of the academic, intellectual skills resulting from a good general education. Whether the actual job techniques beyond this are taught in school or on the job, they cannot be learned if the foundational general education is lacking. The few jobs for which this may not be true are the low-skilled, dead-end jobs which are most vulnerable to technological obsolescence, and if these are the kinds of jobs for which the disadvantaged are trained then they are no better off than before. It is an improved general education, not vocational education in its traditional forms, that must be relied upon to rescue the disadvantaged in our society, and, more importantly, to prevent future generations from growing up as unemployables. This will have to be done unless we are content to tolerate indefinitely a lower class, dependent, substratum in our society, which is unequipped to compete and to succeed in a role of usefulness and dignity within our system.

While occupational education in terms of specific job training may be of limited and short term value to disadvantaged youth, a program of occupational education in the schools which is redirected toward new goals could be of great help to them. The environment in which these young people live does nothing to develop in them a belief in the necessity for work or the possibility of deriving satisfaction from it.[13] They know little about jobs other than the simple and often menial kinds of work done by their neighbors who are fortunate enough to be working at all. Their needs for work orientation, for exposure to many kinds of occupations, and for occupational counseling are even greater than those of middle class youth. Only a comprehensive program of occupational education which is coupled with a really functional general education can help the underprivileged move out of their present disadvantaged state.

The answer to the question, "Can Vocational Education Eliminate Poverty?" is clearly that, by itself, it cannot. Since the schools alone cannot eliminate the conditions which produce the disadvantaged class, vocational education, as only one educational ingredient, surely cannot do so. Furthermore, if occupational education is to be thought of as a form of preparation for a particular job, it may succeed with a few, but it will fail with most unless their general education needs are met. If the more fundamental educational needs of the disadvantaged are satisfied, then occupational education can contribute greatly to their welfare, in the same way that it can serve all others.

The Disadvantaged and the Doctrine of Selectivity

The tendency of vocational educators to favor a selective process in admitting students into their programs has already been referred to. The desire to be selective is in part prompted by a sincere wish to enhance the chances for success by the student in learning the occupation of his choice, and in assuring him employment after training is complete. But another, and equally strong reason for favoring selectivity is to guard the program against the stigma of becoming a "dumping ground" for students who cannot cope with a standard curriculum. Thus there is a conflict between the desire to help the disadvantaged and the wish to improve the image of vocational education. The Vocational Education Act of 1963 singles out the disadvantaged as one of the groups to be served by the programs financed by it, but many vocational leaders have been less than enthusiastic about this aspect of the law. In the 1963 Act no part of the funds were specifically earmarked for the disadvantaged, and when the accomplishments under this law were reviewed by the ad hoc Advisory Council on Vocational Education in 1967 the report stated that the objective of serving disadvantaged youth had hardly been touched. Accordingly, in drafting the 1968 Vocational Education Amendments Act the Congress chose to enforce its wishes by mandating that a fixed percentage of the grants to the states be spent on programs for the disadvantaged. This is now being done, but again without great enthusiasm, for there are still administrators of vocational education who regard the disadvantaged as being outside the responsibility of the regular programs of vocational education.[14]

So long as service to the disadvantaged can be relegated to the Manpower Development and Training programs or those sponsored by other agencies, many vocational educators prefer that they should be, because the disadvantaged individual does not often represent the kind of student who would be chosen if vocational education could select its students. He is, in most respects, the castoff with whom they fear their program has too often been identified in the past. At a time when they see a chance to upgrade the status of occupational education they would like to avoid having their program again associated with the low status student.

In assessing the extent to which occupational education

can benefit the disadvantaged, the conclusion must be that under certain conditions it can be of great value to them, but not as a panacea for all their ills. Occupational education should, in the terms used in the Vocational Education Act of 1963, guarantee that "all persons in all communities . . . will have ready access to vocational training and retraining which is of high quality, which is realistic in the light of actual or anticipated opportunities for employment and which is suited to their needs, interest and ability to profit from such training." If this is taken seriously, the disadvantaged must be included fully in the planning and the implementation of all of the regular programs of vocational education, and the doctrine of selectivity and concern for vocational education's image cannot be allowed to affect their opportunities.

The Responsibility for Remedial Education

The typically low educational attainment of the disadvantaged person (often considerably below his years of schooling) requires that this gap be closed before effective vocational education can help him. Much remedial education may be needed by such students, but vocational educators have generally been reluctant to take the responsibility for it. Just as they often hesitate to include career orientation and planning in their program they also prefer to have the needed compensatory education for the disadvantaged offered elsewhere and to limit their own efforts to the actual job training.

In the case of the disadvantaged this does not work very well. They are not conditioned by their past experience to accept the discipline of prerequisite learning in order to gain deferred benefits. Studies which do not promise an immediate payoff hold little interest for them. Therefore occupational training which includes rather than follows the necessary general education is better suited to their needs. The best programs have succeeded in combining the two so that the student is led to see for himself that he cannot progress in learning the occupation he has selected until he has overcome certain basic deficiencies, and instruction in these is then provided at the exact point where the deficiency becomes an obstacle. This very pragmatic and realistic approach means that the vocational and the general educator must combine their efforts in a very coordinated fashion, and that remedial education cannot become the exclusive responsibility of either. If occupational education is to really serve the disadvantaged the vocational educator must share in helping them to overcome their general education deficiencies.

There are a few examples, chiefly in community colleges, which demonstrate that such an approach can succeed. In these programs disadvantaged students are admitted even though their educational achievement fails to meet minimum requirements, and as they pursue their occupational studies they receive additional, remedial instruction, including individual tutoring, according to their individual needs. They also are provided with special counseling and other services which they may require so that they can learn successfully. Some programs of this kind have had very promising results.

The Occupational Potential of the Disadvantaged

Disadvantaged people cannot compete successfully with those who have achieved a better status unless they are able to use the same keys which others have used to unlock the doors leading to upward mobility. These keys are essentially more and better education, equal access to jobs, and other recognitions to which this education should entitle them. This will not be easily accomplished in a social climate which supports it as an ideal but often denies it in practice. The majority of the disadvantaged do not place much faith in education, partly because they have too often seen its benefits withheld or minimized after members of their group have educated themselves. No one should underestimate the continuing effects of prejudice and discrimination in denying status jobs to the members of the lower classes, and this is not entirely a matter of racial discrimination. Much of what appears to be racial bigotry actually has more of an economic origin. Those who show the most prejudice, particularly with relation to jobs, are often the ones who have most recently reached a somewhat higher economic and social level and who now feel themselves threatened by the possible upward movement of the disadvantaged class.

There is frequently a tendency to make generalized judgments about the thirty or more million people who are at the poverty level in America and to attribute to them low potential, low aspirations and unwillingness to work to improve their own condition. Such generalizations can be very mis-leading. The evidence is that they do not differ basically from other people in their hopes, ambitions, range of intelligence, or potential for improvement. They have as much untapped capacity as those found in more advantaged groups.[15] To allow this capacity to remain unreleased and stifled is surely a tremendous waste of human resources—resources which could be making a useful contribution to society rather than acting as a drain upon it.

Vocational education can become an instrument in breaking the cycle of poverty which leads to unemployment, and thus to more poverty. To try to break this cycle by offering the poor just enough training to get into some kind of employment as quickly as possible is shortsighted and self-defeating; but as part of a truly adequate and uplifting education, devoid of artificial distinctions between academic, general and vocational, and adaptable for each individual, occupational education is a vital resource for meeting the needs of the underclass.

The Disadvantaged and the Image of Vocational Education

The disadvantaged do not, as individuals, always present the attractive image of the idealized student which vocational educators often seek, and which has been described in Chapter 3. On the contrary, their experiences have often caused them to be either passive and indifferent or angry and hostile. Their school experience in particular has probably been one of defeat, and even humiliation. It is easy, therefore, for the vocational educator to feel that their presence in his program only re-enforces the image of vocational education as a second-rate kind of education, designed for low-ability students who can learn only simple, low-status jobs. The fear that occupational education will be demeaned by too much concentration on the disadvantaged is a factor in slowing the introduction of programs for their benefit. On the other hand, the special emphasis upon vocational education as the best means for helping the poor into jobs has carried the connotation that they are not qualified for other forms of education. This has understandably offended many of the underprivileged groups. They feel that if occupational education is low in educational prestige and is considered an alternative for those who cannot succeed in academic studies, to single it out as being especially suitable for them is further evidence of discrimination and inequality. Therefore they reject it.[16] Thus there is rejection on the part of both the vocational education program itself and the disadvantaged who might profit from it, and this only adds to the difficulty of helping them.

Preparing the Disadvantaged For Work

A great deal has been written and spoken on the subject of the special problems of teaching the disadvantaged.[17] Much has been made of some of their supposed characteristics, but there is reason to believe that there are more differences among them than similarities with regard to these character- istics. Like those in other groups, they are all individuals, and even when subjected to essentially the same deprived environ- ment they respond differently to it. One should not rely too heavily upon generalizations or stereotypes in working with the disadvantaged, but rather seek out individual strengths and weaknesses and be guided by them.

Most of the advice on teaching the disadvantaged seems to stress the fact that their daily lives are lived from day to day, with little thought for long term goals, that living, for them is somewhat disorganized, and that they function poorly in the highly structured atmosphere of the school. It is claimed that regularity of attendance and promptness at school or at work is difficult for them to maintain because it is so seldom required in their lives outside of school or work. It is also said that they are not committed to work or to other values which are held by most other Americans. Nevertheless, productive work and other so-called middle class values are closely associated in this society with the rewards desired by the disadvantaged, and if these rewards were more certain for them it might be surprising how quickly they would adopt the values. At any rate, these generalizations do not apply in individual cases, and might be even less common if more individualized teaching strategies were used.

It is true that the disadvantaged have more health problems than other people. They also lack the means for personal privacy as well as some of the other conditions in daily living that are often assumed by teachers who use traditional methods of instruction. An understanding of these things might help vocational teachers, as well as others, to better adjust their work assignments and other demands upon these students. The disadvantaged need more social welfare services than others do to support their efforts to get an education. They also need special insights and sensitivity on the part of those who teach them, for they have not the means to cope with their problems as well as do those with more resources. Needs which among the more fortunate would normally be met by the family or by the student himself must often be provided for in other ways for the student from an impoverished environment. At the same time most of these deprived students are sensitive and embarrassed about their poor background, and they resent any form of condescension.

One suggestion which is made with regard to teaching the disadvantaged, many of whom are deficient in dealing with verbal symbols in speech, in reading and in writing, is that teachers should use nonverbal methods and materials. This may be advisable in the early stages of learning, but unless it is accompanied by remedial instruction to improve verbal ability it will only serve to further handicap the student. Under actual job conditions he will have to function at the level of reading and speech which the work requires, for special, nonverbal ways of communication are not used in the real world of work. This is why it is so important that the disadvantaged student not be permitted to remain educationally retarded and why most of his instruction must be geared to standard levels of reading and speech.

One mistake which has been made by vocational educators and by others in their attempts to serve the disadvantaged is to segregate them from other students and thus label them as being different or inferior. Because they are usually educationally retarded they are likely to be treated as a separate group, not qualified to learn side by side with others of their age group.[18] In large cities the school authorities have sometimes reopened abandoned school buildings or rented space in commercial buildings and used them as skill centers for the occupational training of the disadvantaged. Once again this introduces a form of separation which is a constant reminder to these students of their educational and social shortcomings. While this may be done with the best of intentions, it fails to meet a most important need of the disadvantaged—the need to be a part of the larger society from which they have too long been isolated. The needs of the disadvantaged for occupational education should be met by including them in the same educational setting that is shared by all other students, and by caring for their special needs as individuals, not as a group. One result of the great new concern for the disadvantaged which has developed, and a result which is not to their benefit, has been to create an institution of them as a class and new professional careers for serving them. What they need most is to become assimilated into society at large, sharing equally in its advantages, and this will scarcely be accomplished by continuing to treat them as a group apart.

Summary

A part of the American people, now estimated to include as much as 20 percent of the population, is so economically and socially deprived that to a large extent it is forced to exist outside the mainstream of American society. In recent years these people have become so increasingly visible that their condition has become intolerable in an affluent society and is the cause of much public concern. The minority racial and ethnic groups are heavily represented among them, and the term disadvantaged is frequently used to identify them.

Although a great many of the disadvantaged are too old or too young for the labor force, a widespread belief has developed that the way to end the poverty which is at the root of their condition is to make them employable through job training. Accordingly, there has been a great deal of official emphasis upon occupational education as a major part of the solution to this urgent social problem. It is most important to rescue as many as possible of the adult victims of poverty by helping them into stable employment but it is equally essential that the children and youth from this group not be allowed to reach a condition which makes them unemployable.

The problem is a complex one and does not yield to simple or single types of solutions. Experience has already shown that direct job training for the disadvantaged is largely ineffective unless it is supported by a base of general education. It is further complicated by racial and ethnic discrimination in education and in employment practices. Vocational education alone is not the answer to poverty, but it can make a contribution to relieving the condition of the poor. Vocational educators have been reluctant to accept the disadvantaged into their programs because of their need for a great deal of remedial education and also because of the fear that they may add to the image of vocational education as a program suitable chiefly for academic failures. The doctrine of selectivity, which is favored by many vocational educators, conflicts with the openness which is required if the disadvantaged are to be served. Because the disadvantaged are typically retarded in their general education, vocational education must accept part of the responsibility for the compensatory instruction needed to remedy this deficiency so that they can succeed in their occupational studies.

At the same time, the entire educational enterprise must so revise its ways of educating youth that a poor environment will not continue to result in almost certain educational retardation and failure. The need for patching up educational deficiencies must be eliminated. The potential of the children of the poor to achieve a satisfactory level of education, to prepare for vocations at all levels, and to join the mainstream of American life is as great as the potential of any other group.

The hesitation on the part of vocational educators to welcome and serve the disadvantaged is matched by an equal reluctance on the part of the poor to become identified with vocational education. They resent the fact that there is such a widespread feeling that vocational training is the only form of education of which they are capable. They think of it as leading only to low-skilled, menial jobs. Attitudes on both sides must be changed if the disadvantaged are to profit from occupational education.

Many recommendations have been made for specialized techniques for teaching the disadvantaged. Some of them can be helpful, but many others are questionable. They may lead to isolation and segregation of the disadvantaged in the educational process, but there is no evidence that learning comes to them in ways which differ from the learning processes of others.

REFERENCES

1. Harrington, Michael. *The Other America*. New York: Macmillan Co., 1962.
2. National Committee on the Employment of Youth. *A Guide to the Development of Vocational Education Programs and Services for the Disadvantaged*. New York: National Committee on the Employment of Youth, 1970.

882

282

8888

88

3. Evans, Rupert; Mangum, Garth; and Pragan, Otto. *Education for Employment.* Institute of Labor and Industrial Relations. Ann Arbor: The University of Michigan, 1969.
4. Ibid.
5. Western New York School Development Council. *The Nature of Poverty in Chautauqua County, New York.* Buffalo: State University of New York, 1966.
6. Hill, H. "Employment, Manpower Training and the Black Worker." *Journal of Negro Education* (Summer, 1969).
7. U. S. Congress. *Manpower Development and Training Act.*
8. U. S. Congress. *Vocational Education Act of 1963.*
9. U. S. Congress. *Elementary and Secondary Education Act of 1965.* Public Law 89-10, 89th Cong., 1965.
10. U. S. Congress. *Economic Opportunity Act of 1964.* Public Law 88-452, 88th Cong., 1964.
11. U. S. Congress. *Vocational Education Amendments Act of 1968.*
12. National Advisory Council on Vocational Education. *First Annual Report.*
13. National Committee on the Employment of Youth. *A Guide to the Development of Vocational Education Programs and Services for the Disadvantaged.*
14. Evans, Mangum, and Pragan. *Education for Employment.*
15. National Committee on the Employment of Youth. *A Guide to the Development of Vocational Education Programs and Services for the Disadvantaged.*
16. Knoell. *Toward Educational Opportunities for All.*
17. Kemp. *The Youth We Haven't Served.*
18. Venn, Grant. *Man, Education and Manpower.* Washington, D. C.: American Association of School Administrators, 1970.

CHAPTER 9

OCCUPATIONAL EDUCATION AND ITS STATUS

Occupational Education and Its Image

One of the issues which continually recurs in relation to occupational education is the question of the public and educational attitudes toward it. Those engaged in it frequently charge that these attitudes are both negative and unfair, and they urge that parents, students, and their colleagues in education should acknowledge the merits of vocational education and accord it the same prestige as other forms of education. The first report of the permanent National Advisory Council on Vocational Education was devoted entirely to this theme.[1] It seemed to be saying that unless the public attitude toward occupational education undergoes a complete and dramatic change, the future of the program is limited.

In reality, vocational education has different images in different places, and in the eyes of different observers. As a result of her study Knoell reports that technical graduates are well prepared for further education but that vocational graduates are often poorly prepared for either a job or for further education.[2] Kohler also gave vocational education a poor rating as a result of her study of the New York City vocational high schools.[3] On the other hand Conant found another large city where the vocational program was well received and popular.[4] Yet the idea persists that vocational education lacks the status and prestige that it deserves and that this reputation must somehow be overcome so that it can enjoy an appeal equal to that of college preparatory education. The status of occupational education is related in part to the status of the occupations which it serves, and while it may seem strange that a highly industrial society would not place the highest value upon occupations most vital to its economy, the prestige of occupations does not seem to rest upon these grounds.

The Problem of Occupational Status

The existence of differences in social status based upon occupation has a long history in organized society. It has undergone many changes during that time and has taken different forms in different cultures, depending upon the dominant values which have evolved in each. Throughout most cultures, however, less social prestige has been accorded to those who perform the manual and more routine tasks of society than to those who either do intellectual work or acquire power through conquest or through inheritance. In early societies those who attained higher status were able to gain it through force of arms, or by being well born, and they became the rulers and leaders, while others performed the daily tasks of life either as slaves or serfs. In oriental cultures, which have the longest history of cilivization, intellectual pursuits and the occupations to which they lead have traditionally been given the greatest respect. The Athenian Greeks prized learning so highly that they gave it first place in their scheme of values, and considered the artisan, the farmer, and other workers unworthy to become free citizens. Western Europe evolved a social organization in which status was largely identified with occupation, which was in turn related to family status, and even in England, where equal political rights for everyone have long prevailed, strong social class stratification based upon birth and occupation has persisted down to the present time.

From the beginning of the American experience there has been a strong tradition of egalitarianism which has helped to create the goal of a classless society as a national ideal. Those who framed the political structure of the United States and wrote its constitution did everything possible to prevent class distinctions based upon birth and they refused to permit the creation of any sort of royalty or of a titled class. Yet every thoughtful American knows that a hierarchy of social class exists in this country and that it is closely related to occupations. What has been accomplished in the United States is a degree of economic and social, and therefore status, mobility which is greater than that to be found in almost any other society. Nevertheless, all occupations possess varying degrees of prestige, and these are not entirely related to the financial rewards which they carry. To be unemployed is to enjoy the lowest status of all but for those who are employed some occupations clearly bestow more prestige upon the worker than do others. Until recently plumbers were better paid than college professors, but in all public polls which rank occupational status, the professors were placed much higher. Supreme court justices top the list in occupational prestige in most such rankings, much higher than business executives whose salaries are much greater.[5]

At levels above the underprivileged, social stratification in the United States is less sharp and more fluid than in almost any other western country, but nevertheless it exists, and it is related to occupations. Studies indicate that there is a general consensus among Americans as to the prestige value of various kinds of occupations and these studies also suggest that there are four factors which enter into the prestige ranking which the public gives to occupations. These factors are the economic returns of the occupation, its social contribution, the amount of education and training it requires, and the extent to which it deals with intellectual matters. These factors seem to carry equal weight in establishing the prestige of an occupation.[6]

Occupational Status and Occupational Education

Vocational education early placed limitations upon the occupations with which it wished to be identified, and these, as included in the Smith-Hughes law, were confined to a small segment of the manual occupations related to farming and manufacturing. The same law prohibited vocational education from conducting collegiate level instruction. The discussion in Chapter 1 brought out the fact that those who founded the vocational education movement in America were greatly motivated by a social welfare philosophy of serving the working classes, but the occupations on which they chose to concentrate are not those with high social prestige. The higher prestige occupations are those having a greater intellectual component and requiring higher education. Yet from the beginning, vocational educators have continually complained about the lack of respect by the public for the kind of education which they were conducting. Much time has been spent in deploring the poor image of vocational education and in urging the public, and particularly other educators to consider it more favorably. Indeed, there is so much anxiety about this on the part of many vocational educators that it seems to have developed into a full fledged inferiority complex with some of them.[7]

It has already been shown that this feeling of inferiority and the resentment it has generated among vocational educators began early in the history of vocational education, and that it was attributed to the snobbery of the educated class toward the manual worker. Yet in a society such as ours, where the educated class is not an elite, but includes nearly everyone, this argument can have little weight. The actual image of vocational education must be largely what vocational educators have made it, for they have had more centralized control over their program for a longer period of time than any other group of educators has ever had. By constantly lamenting what they believe to be the unfavorable image of vocational education they may have done more than their detractors to perpetuate that image. The movement began with a strong commitment to serving the needs of the lower social classes, and it took pride in doing so. At that time it did not demand any particular level of prestige, but very quickly the problem of educational parity arose and it still remains as a source of difficulty in the minds of many.

The Obsession With Image and Prestige

To a detached observer, reading the current utterances of vocational education leaders, it would appear that far too much importance is attached by them to the question of vocational education's prestige. It is an overstressed issue, which has become almost an obsession, to the point where it detracts from the positive and necessary contributions which occupational education could and should be making. The future of occupational education depends much less upon its image than upon its performance.

This undue concern with prestige continues to be expressed in several ways. There is the charge that vocational education is the victim of bad and misleading publicity. Actually, the opposite is true. By far the greater part of the publicity about vocational education which appears in the press and elsewhere is favorable, and only rarely is anything published that is adverse. As a concept it has more support in Congress, in state legislatures, and from general educators than ever before.

Some vocational leaders still attempt to build up occupational education by minimizing the value of general and liberal education. They attack the college entrance programs as being worthless for those who do not go to college, not recognizing that the major part of such a curriculum consists of the general education which is basic to all jobs and to intelligent citizenship. If such a curriculum had no value in the job market, as some vocational enthusiasts suggest, the unemployment rate would be astronomical. This downgrading of academic education is a heritage from times long past when some academic educators were disdainful of vocational education and reluctant to include it as an essential ingredient in a complete education, but this situation no longer prevails. Modern educators accept the need for occupational education and are anxious to include it in their programs. What they sometimes cannot accept is the limited concept of occupational education that is still held by some vocational educators. The leading academic educators in the country have endorsed occupational education, and there is surely no conspiracy in academic circles to discredit it.[8, 9, 10]

Vocational educators often express resentment that their programs are considered to be an inferior form of education, but it is only when they offer narrow programs, limited to specific job training, rather than open-ended programs of career education that their value is questioned. In today's world every informed educator, parent or student is aware of the need for a complete, broad education, properly balanced between liberal studies and career preparation, and they will not accept less.

Concern with the prestige of occupational education exists not only with respect to academic education, but also between different forms of vocational education. There are some very interesting forms of status consciousness within the vocational movement itself. The term vocational-technical education is widely used as a name for one type of occupational education but its exact meaning is not always clear. It is often taken to mean vocational *and* technical education, with a real distinction implied between the two. Those involved in technical education are careful to maintain this distinction, and tend to regard their programs as somewhat superior to those of a vocational nature, and in this usage the term vocational seems to connote manual or trade education. Technical educators tend to disassociate themselves from vocational education. In the minds of many, technical education, because it deals largely with science and mathematics and sends its students on to associate and baccalaureate degrees, becomes more identified with academic education, and therefore enjoys more status. Similarly, programs of cooperative work-study education have less prestige in the eyes of some vocational educators than the more traditional full-time programs.

Teachers of many vocational subjects earn a college degree as a part of their regular preparation for teaching, and their professional credentials do not differ from those of most academic teachers. Those who teach trades or other industrial occupations, however, are usually recruited directly from their industrial occupations and often lack a college education. Although many of them later earn a college degree, as a group they are most sensitive to their lack of academic standing and they are often convinced that academic teachers, counselors and others have less regard for them as teachers because of their different background. They sometimes react by questioning the value of a college education as a requirement for teaching, by claiming that too many students go to college, and by feeling that as teachers they do not receive proper professional recognition. It would be very difficult to document any of these beliefs. Good teachers respect professional competence, and they extend this respect to the expert vocational teacher regardless of his academic attainments. Since educational requirements for all kinds of jobs are rising it is only to be expected that all teachers, including vocational teachers will in the future earn a college degree as a part of their professional preparation. In the meantime there is little evidence that the lack of academic credentials by some vocational teachers lowers the image of occupational education.

Is the Baccalaureate Degree Overemphasized?

In defending the status of occupational education its practitioners still tend to think of it as being non-college in character. In their desire to attract more and better students they therefore criticize what they consider to be an overemphasis upon college attendance and question the aspirations of the increasing number of youth and their parents who set their sights upon a baccalaureate degree. They contend that many of these students should elect to follow a vocational curriculum, with the implication that they should end their education with high school. They point to the high attrition rates in colleges and seem to suggest that those who fail to complete their college programs should have somehow been headed off at an earlier point and not permitted to try. By the same logic, of course, those who fail to complete high school should not have been allowed to enter it.

This whole line of reasoning which tries to de-emphasize college and the earning of a degree in favor of taking vocational training is counter-productive in the attempt to make occupational education more attractive. The striving for a college education is a natural outcome of the demands of technology on the one hand and the affluence created by technology on the other, coupled with the traditional American drive for upward social mobility rather than social stratification. A college education obviously pays off in income and in status, and more and more young people are going to aspire to it, whether they achieve a baccalaurate degree or not. There are very practical and worthy reasons which impel many of today's youth and their parents to reach for higher education, and there is nothing to indicate that this will soon change.

We frequently read expressions from public figures, including some educators, that there are too many going to college, too many working for degrees who are not really interested in them, too many who are not capable of meeting the intellectual demands of a college program. There is much confusion about this. There are, of course, students attending college for reasons other than intellectual growth. There always have been, even when few attended college. Of those who do not finish, and many will not, most will leave for reasons other than lack of capacity. The scarcity of available jobs for youth has already been noted, and some form of education beyond the high school is increasingly the only alternative to idleness for many. This may not be the most desirable reason for staying in school but until the adult groups which control employment are ready to make the concessions necessary to open up the job market to youth and to share with the schools the social responsibility for providing a place in the world of work for these young people, school will be better than idleness. Occupational education can make one of its most important social contributions at this very point by concentrating the greater part of its resources at the post high school level. It is a mistake to lump all post high school education together under the term college. This, to most people, means a four-year, liberal arts school of some kind. There can be many avenues for further education that are neither four years in length nor completely liberal arts in content. Fortunately, these opportunities are increasing, but not fast enough.

In some ways perhaps the baccalaureate degree is over-emphasized, but in the larger sense the American public is sound in its judgment that everyone should get all the education he can. Education is one of the indispensable keys to a better life, and vocational education cannot improve its own image by questioning the value of getting more of it. If occupational education has been unattractive to many because its students have been unable to qualify for further education, this is on the way to being remedied, and in the future its programs must not be permitted to so restrict the further education of its graduates.

Public Attitudes and Public Relations

As much as vocational educators have protested what they believe to be an unjustified lack of prestige for their programs, they have seldom suggested any positive steps to increase it. They have, instead, placed the onus for the alleged low status upon others, chiefly the academic minded. They have not always been willing to examine critically their own policies to determine whether there are any shortcomings which might account for such an attitude, and they have tended to resent outside critics who have attempted to suggest reforms. The response to low prestige has more often been to condemn the critics, to exhort the educators and the public to change their attitudes, and to imply that this can be accomplished by some sort of massive public relations effort.

It is frequently claimed that general educators, counselors, and the public do not understand vocational education and are therefore negative toward it, but there is nothing about the concept of occupational education that cannot be easily understood, if confusing technicalities are not insisted upon. Vocational educators have sometimes confused the public, their fellow educators, and even themselves by creating technical distinctions and differences between their programs which are often contrived and which are of little real importance outside the ranks of the purists. The hazy difference between industrial arts and other kinds of industrial education is one example of this, but hundreds of hours and thousands of words have been devoted to drawing up lists of criteria to distinguish between them. The differences between technical education and vocational education are unclear and trivial and of interest only to certain specialists. To some vocationalists it is very important to differentiate between diversified cooperative vocational education, work-study education, and work-experience education, but they cannot expect other educators or the public to try to understand such technicalities. The distinctions between homemaking, wage earning homemaking and vocational homemaking represent another example of artificial and needless differences. In view of the pressing need for extending occupational education in its broader context, such distinctions seem to others as esoteric and irrelevant as academic hairsplitting.

Attitudes of the public toward social institutions vary to the degree that these institutions serve to satisfy the values which are most prized by the society. Some superficial attitudes can perhaps be modified by a public relations approach, but those that concern long and deeply held beliefs are not so easily changed. This applies to the image of occupational education. Public relations techniques will not change it. Only as occupational education realigns itself to the demands of a society in rapid change, and accepts rather than resists the new role that this calls for will it gain the higher status that it could have and that it has sought so long.

Improving the Image of Vocational Education

The image of occupational education will always be formed by what those outside its own ranks observe about it, not by what its proponents think they should believe. Like any other worthy movement it can and should present its best achievements to the public, but its acceptance and the respect with which it is regarded must ultimately rest upon how well it truly fulfills its educational function in terms of society as it is, not as it used to be. Vocational education will be perceived by others pretty much as it is perceived and directed by its own leaders. If those who lead and speak for it view it chiefly as a job training program and as a means for satisfying the needs of the labor market, then it will, in the public mind, be thought of as just another form of manpower training, like those conducted by the Department of Labor and other government agencies. It will be respected for what it is, and to a certain degree supported, but it will not be regarded as real education and not many young people will be attracted to it. On the other hand if occupational education changes its own image of itself by accepting broad, career oriented goals, by reducing its emphasis upon first job skills and by a fusion with education at large, then it will be recognized as truly educational. It will then receive acceptance and approval as a part of the institution of education rather than as an agency of training.

One of several things which can help to bring this about is for vocational education to join the educational establishment rather than to continue to function as the vocational education establishment. This means combining forces with the many other branches of American education, sharing common resources, espousing and supporting common educational causes, actively participating in the same professional organizations and, in short, becoming educators first and vocational educators second. Until this happens occupational education will not share in whatever status and prestige which education at large may enjoy.

Summary

Those engaged in occupational education have long been unhappy because they believe that their programs suffer from low prestige in the eyes of educators, students and the public. This anxiety about status has probably overemphasized the real importance of the issue and has diverted time and energy from other and more vital problems facing vocational education. Occupational education has developed a sort of institutional inferiority complex which may, like a self-fulfilling prophecy, have helped to create the very attitudes it deplores.

The undue concern for status has led to unnecessary and unproductive reactions on the part of vocational educators. Among these are an unwarranted suspicion of the academic community, attacks on the value of general and academic education and criticism of collegiate and other forms of education beyond the high school. There has been a tendency on the part of some vocational educators to disparage the baccalaureate degree and to suggest that general liberal education is overvalued and overemphasized. There appear to be two motives for such reactions. One is a defensive response by those who feel themselves to be the victims of intellectual snobbishness. The other is to help their own program to grow by discouraging students from attempting to enter college or other forms of post high school education and to elect terminal vocational high school training instead. There is little prospect that status can be raised or program growth accomplished by such means.

Although the image of occupational education is not as unfavorable as many vocationalists appear to believe, they usually attempt to explain it by blaming others rather than by examining their own practices in order to learn what might account for it. Instead they call upon others to change their attitudes and to elevate the status of occupational education by eliminating the presumed prejudice through a process of thought changing. The usual suggestion for doing this is through some form of public relations, but it is doubtful that any attitudes will be changed by either propaganda or exhortation. Vocationalists have charged that other educators do not understand their programs, but by creating distinctions within distinctions they themselves have unnecessarily complicated these programs so that there is confusion even within their own ranks about terminology and purposes.

If the image of occupational education needs to be improved, what will help most is for it to become really an integral part of American education, not an appendage or a separate enterprise. This will require it to accommodate to the larger goals and share in the larger problems of education and will demand that vocational educators become educators first and vocational specialists second.

REFERENCES

1. Report of the National Advisory Council on Vocational Education (December, 1968).
2. Knoell. *Toward Educational Opportunities for All.*
3. Kohler. *Youth and Work in New York City.*

4. Conant. *The American High School Today.*
5. Hatt, Paul, and North, C. C. *Man, Work and Society,* ed. Nosow, W., and Form, W. New York: Basic Books, Inc., 1962.
6. Davies, A. F. *Man, Work and Society,* ed. Nosow, W. and Form, W. New York: Basic Books, Inc. 1962.
7. Workman. "Schoolmen Blamed for Image Problem." *American Vocational Journal.*
8. Conant. *The American High School Today.*
9. Draper. *Educating for Work.*
10. National Advisory Council on Vocational Education. *Vocational Education: The Bridge Between Man and His Work.*

CHAPTER 10

TEACHERS AND LEADERS FOR OCCUPATIONAL EDUCATION

The Need For Teachers and Leaders

The recruitment and preparation of teachers for occupational subjects and the selection and development of administrators and other leaders have been continuing problems since vocational education was first introduced into the public schools. Even though the number of occupational categories included in most programs of vocational education has been small, they were sufficiently diverse to require many subject matter specialists in order to meet the demands of the vocational curriculums. This meant that there could be little common technical content in vocational teacher preparation, as would be the case of teachers of academic subjects. What is more important in shaping the character of the program, the philosophy which has prevailed has precluded the joint preparation of vocational teachers with teachers of other subjects, or even with other vocational teachers, and this has served to perpetuate further the separatism of vocational education from the rest of the educational world.[1] It has even tended to isolate vocational teachers from one another. For example, on a college campus where vocational teachers are prepared there may be no contact between those preparing to teach agricultural subjects, those preparing to teach industrial subjects, and those preparing to teach business subjects. Teachers of elementary subjects, of English, mathematics, science, music, physical education and other specialties often pursue at least part of their professional studies together, in common courses, as professional educators. Vocational teachers seldom share these experiences, but instead receive their professional preparation in separate courses, apart from their colleagues in other areas of education.

The Smith-Hughes Act recognized the need for an adequate supply of teachers and it authorized the use of federal funds for teacher training, and for the training of leaders. Some of the subsequent federal legislation continued this support, and the Vocational Education Amendments Act of 1968, by amending the Higher Education Act, provides for the expansion of such training through leadership development awards for full-time advanced study and by grants to encourage the preparation and upgrading of vocational teachers.[2] Nevertheless, many of the earlier problems remain, and it is doubtful whether they can be solved without a fresh approach to the whole question of how vocational teachers and leaders should be prepared.

The root of the problem is the decision as to what constitutes appropriate qualifications and appropriate preparation for vocational teachers and for those who will have leadership roles in occupational education. This in turn relates directly to what the goals of occupational education are thought to be. If the goal is simply to train each student for an entry job, then the emphasis in teacher qualifications will be upon occupational skills, because there is little need for intellectual breadth or depth in such a program. On the other hand if the broader goals of occupational breadth, versatility, adaptability and learning how to learn are considered to be more important, then the teacher's occupational skills will become subordinate to his possession of a broad and balanced education.

If occupational education is to expand as it should in order to meet the needs of most Americans, rather than serving a small minority, it will need many more teachers and leaders in the years ahead. Unless it accepts more comprehensive goals than it has in the past, it will not grow, because it will not be widely accepted, and there will be no great problem in finding the teachers that will be required. For the growth that should and must come, however, a new breed of teachers and a new breed of leaders will have to be developed, and in numbers well beyond what present sources can supply.

Traditional Patterns of Teacher Preparation

The preparation and certification of vocational teachers and leaders has long been a responsibility of the individual states. This has led to variations in the qualifications adopted by different states, although the overshadowing control by the federal authorities through legislation and administrative codes has maintained certain basic similarities. In general, the task of preparation has been assigned to the colleges and universities within the states, including the land-grant colleges. These colleges have provided pre-service programs on their own campuses, and often through extension courses at other locations throughout the state. They have also conducted much in-service education through evening, summer, and regular sessions. A feature which has been unique to vocational education has been the use of itinerant teacher trainers who are members of a college staff but who travel throughout the state giving individual assistance and supervision to vocational teachers. High school vocational teachers must meet the certification requirements which the state prescribes for teaching their subject, but for some vocational teachers these are less demanding than for academic teachers. No certification requirements are imposed in most states for teachers of post secondary occupational subjects.

The pre-service preparation of vocational teachers varies according to the field of specialization, and although the Vocational Education Act of 1963 in effect abolished the traditional service categories, teacher preparation is still conducted in terms of the Smith-Hughes philosophy of emphasis upon occupations to be served. Thus teachers of agriculture are trained in land-grant colleges where their studies are divided between technical subjects in agriculture and general liberal courses, plus the professional education courses required for certification. This leads to a degree in agricultural education. The same is true for teachers of homemaking, with the appropriate differences in technical content. Teachers of business subjects must hold a degree in business education, which is a combination of studies in business practice, general liberal subjects and professional education. Distributive education teachers follow a college program leading to a degree in marketing, with additional work in education. Teachers of nursing receive their professional training in approved schools of nursing and supplement their degree with postgraduate or in-service courses in education.

Teachers of other health occupations also receive their occupational training by earning an associate or a baccalaureate degree in their specialty, plus clinical experience. Since most of them teach at the post high school level, their professional education for teaching is usually an in-service form of training, and differs considerably with individuals. This is also true of technical teachers, whose basic subject competence results from earning a degree in some scientific or technical field.

It is axiomatic that to teach well one must have a thorough knowledge of his subject, although in today's world, without constant updating, such knowledge is soon obsolete. For the great majority of its teachers vocational education has relied upon systematic study in collegiate programs leading to a degree to provide this knowledge. It is true that token amounts of practical experience are sometimes required for some of them, but the one or two years of such experience that are sometimes demanded of teachers of distributive subjects, health subjects and technical subjects are largely a gesture toward the theory that experience as a worker is essential for vocational teaching. Surely such brief experience cannot add much to the subject matter competence of these teachers. Teachers of office practice are not typically required to have any employment experience, yet in general they have been very successful.

It is chiefly in the trade and industrial subjects that teachers are recruited directly from the occupation itself, with no college training or degree and with no prior plans or preparation for teaching. Although this field enrolls a minority of all vocational students, it tends to dominate the thinking of the overall program of occupational education and has been the most impervious to change. Trade and industrial educators have long insisted that the necessary subject competence can only be attained by lengthy experience on the job and that to secure such teachers it is necessary to forego formal education in favor of occupational experience, and convert craftsmen into teachers. The theory that the only way to know enough about an occupation to teach it is to work at it over an extended period of time has long been supported by many vocational educators. An analysis shows that only in the field of trade and industrial education has it actually been applied. In this field the amount of work experience considered necessary has varied from as little as three years in some states to as much as nine years in others, which in itself indicates the lack of agreement as to exactly what contribution to teaching success such experience is expected to make.

Occupational Experience and the Vocational Teacher

The priority upon practical experience as a requirement for vocational teaching goes back to the early days of the vocational program and reflects early emphasis upon specific job training and mechanical performance as the chief goal of the vocational teacher. Given this goal, it was argued that although these skills were being developed in prospective teachers in some public and private institutions and colleges, their graduates could not transmit to their students the actual working atmosphere of the shop or factory and therefore the students would not be employable. This theory was never subjected to research but nevertheless it prevailed, in spite of evidence to the contrary in other fields of vocational education. It has led to many problems and has contributed to the separatism and the status consciousness that still hinder the full development of occupational education.

The quality of a learning experience is by no means easy to measure, but if a field of study is mastered in a program offered by an approved college or university, some recognized standards have been met. Such institutions are subject to program review and to common accreditation standards which include quality of staff, facilities and curriculum. No such standards exist by which to appraise the quality of the learning experience when it is acquired on the job and prior to any plans for teaching. Five years of employment may mean five years of varied and valuable experience or it may mean one year of experience repeated five times. Vocational educators have recognized this and have attempted to evaluate the breadth of the experience of those accepted as teachers by the use of trade competency tests. Still, there are no accepted norms which can be applied in such tests and this has led to heavy reliance upon the length of occupational experience as the principal criterion for judging competence.

By demanding a rather lengthy occupational experience as a basic qualification for teaching, recruitment must usually be from among persons who are older than most who enter the teaching profession, and who have had no previous plans for such a career. In itself this should not be a handicap, but they find themselves with a minimum of formal education in a profession where a college degree is the norm and where such a degree is required of most other vocational teachers. In many states trade and industrial teachers can become fully certified without a degree, but for personal and professional satisfaction many of them desire to earn one. It is usually possible to do this, but only by many years of part-time study during which family and teaching responsibilities compete for their time and financial resources. This has led, in some cases, to the creation of degree programs which emphasize technical content at the expense of liberal studies and which result in a narrow and specialized education that further identifies the vocational teacher in his own mind with his own specialty rather than with a broader spectrum of education.

The lack of advanced education and the lack of balance in degree programs for industrial teachers has helped to increase the feelings of inferiority and apartness which were discussed in Chapter 9. Too many vocational teachers have had too little opportunity to share their training and their thinking with teachers in other fields and to test their own ideas against those of others in the intellectual marketplace. This makes them unduly sensitive to their lack of academic credentials. This sensitivity is well illustrated by the recent action of a group of industrial teachers in one state in proposing that vocational teachers who lack a degree but are certified to teach be automatically awarded a degree by one of the colleges of that state.[3] This of course would not improve the quality of their teaching and might even lower their status in the eyes of fellow teachers, but it does indicate the extent to which the problem of collegiate training remains as a difficulty in the preparation of some vocational teachers. It is possible, of course, to earn a degree without becoming educated, but it is to be hoped that this would be rare among those whose profession is education. It is unlikely that the members of any profession can, in the future, enter that profession without at least a baccalaureate degree, and vocational education must soon meet this standard for all of its teachers as it now does for most of them. This is not to glorify the possession of a degree nor merely to match the paper credentials of other teachers. It is simply to recognize that teaching, like other professions, has now reached a point where it requires advanced education which goes well beyond subject matter competence alone if students are to be prepared for effective living, learning and working.

The question is not whether occupational teachers should be competent in the subjects they teach, for this is accepted by all, but whether long term employment is the only means for developing such competence. Because of the deep traditional commitment to this one device, alternatives have not only been unexplored but have been frowned upon. It is now necessary that new ways be found to produce the competent, broadly educated vocational teachers that the future demands.

Liberal Education and the Vocational Teacher

In planning for the preparation of vocational teachers for the future we cannot escape the question which was discussed in Chapter 5 of balance in the educational process. Collegiate programs in engineering, business administration and other special areas formerly were heavily loaded with technical content, with a minimum of general studies, the humanities, the behavioral sciences or social sciences. It was found that the products of such programs often proved to be excellent technicians, but that this was the limit of their competence. They could not relate their special skills to the larger social, economic and human contexts in which they were called upon to function. Accordingly, some years ago, these curriculums were modified to include a great deal more general liberal education.

Too many vocational teachers suffer from the same imbalance in their education. As teachers they need to understand modern technology as a powerful new force in the world, not just as a proliferation of remarkable new hardware. They need to understand the impact of technology on social change, economic change, political change, value change, human development and cultural patterns. It may be said that other teachers also lack these understandings, and this is true. All teachers need a broad and liberal education as a foundation for whatever specialty they may follow.

Teachers can no longer think of themselves as simply transmitters of skills and facts which they themselves have acquired. Learning how to learn will be the most important lesson that students of the future can master and the student whose learning is limited only to what his teacher knows will be unable to cope with the world beyond the schoolroom. The interrelationship of knowledge and the effects of discoveries in one field upon developments in others are important to students whose future lives will be lived in a world in which technology is more pervasive than even we have known. It is imperative that teachers of occupational subjects be educated to understand what this means in areas beyond those of their own technical specialty.

The practice of creating vocational teachers by finding a craftsman or technician who can be persuaded to teach and converting him into a teacher by exposure to a few courses in education leaves him without the educational foundation for becoming a professional career teacher. There are those, of course, who feel that the liberal studies are of little value for the vocational teacher and that to include them in his preparation is only a concession to academia. This viewpoint still has its advocates among vocational educators. It presumes that vocational instructors are essentially job trainers rather than professional teachers, and that their function resembles that of a foreman breaking in a new worker in a factory. But a school is expected to educate, not merely train, and its teachers must be of a different caliber altogether than the industrial trainer.

Is the Craftsman-Teacher Concept Outmoded?

Years ago the engineering colleges abandoned the practice of employing skilled craftsmen with little formal education to teach some of the mechanical processes of industrial production to freshmen in their engineering programs. They found that these specifics could be learned in much less time and in better relation to the future engineer's needs by using other methods and professional personnel. The time has probably come to take the same step in the selection and preparation of vocational industrial teachers and to substitute other means for the time honored practice of converting established craftsmen into teachers. We have long since abandoned the idea of preparing physicians by apprenticing practical healers to doctors or of having lawyers learn their profession by reading law or of creating engineers by practical training on the job. Teaching makes as many demands upon the trained intellect and calls for as much formal preparation as do any of these professions and the kind and length of preparation which teachers should have is not compatible with the limitations imposed by trying to develop a craftsman into a teacher. The teacher whose principal asset is a long experience as a worker can bring to his task only what he knows about that occupation at the time he left it. Many such teachers do try to keep up with new developments in their field but this is extraordinarily difficult for them to do while trying to catch up professionally with other teachers who have gained their professional training before beginning to teach.

The Vocational Education Act of 1963 shifted the instructional emphasis from specific occupations to job clusters or families of occupations, and the Vocational Education Amendments Act of 1968 further strengthened this trend. The emphasis on narrow preparation for job entry with a priority on high levels of skill proficiency is being changed to the development of versatility and flexibility. Many vocational educators do not agree with this and try to resist such change, but the intent of Congress is clear and is based on the recommendations of the Advisory Council on Vocational Education of 1967. This will have profound consequences upon the qualifications of future vocational industrial teachers and will greatly reduce the need for the depth skills which have been the major asset of the craftsman-teacher.

Whatever alternatives may be devised to replace the process of bringing skilled craftsmen into vocational education as teachers, they will have to assure four things—necessary occupational skill competence, a broad liberal education, full professional development and a baccalaureate degree which will mean educational parity with other teachers. Future teachers must also be able to enter such programs on a career preparation basis rather than by leaving another occupation to do so.[4] Although the older system has produced many excellent teachers in the past, it must now give way to new ways of developing teachers for the new era which occupational education is now entering. To acknowledge this in no way detracts from the fine contributions of those who have taught in the past and who came into teaching after a career in industry. We still honor the many elementary teachers who were the products of the one-year normal schools of earlier days, although they could not qualify to teach in today's schools.

Teacher Qualifications and Program Goals

Occupational teachers for tomorrow's schools will have to be prepared for differentiated tasks so that they can meet the revised curriculum goals of a re-directed program of occupational education. Teachers will be needed who can successfully reach the varying goals that will emerge for differing levels of education and different stages of student maturity. Some of these objectives are not presently to be found in the curriculum or they appear only in embryonic form in a few places, but they must ultimately become a part of the curriculum of all pupils from the elementary years onward. They will require teachers with skill and imagination and with special preparation for providing career orientation without being guidance counselors. Such curricular innovations, for example as the Introduction to Vocations Program in New Jersey[5] and the Technology for Children program based upon Scobey's book, *Teaching Children About Technology*[6] are forerunners of a part of the future occupational curriculum which will become as common as science and mathematics in the school curriculum. At these elementary levels it will probably be more effective to include the necessary subject material in the pre-service or in-service preparation of the elementary teacher, but occupational educators will have to be thoroughly involved in doing this. The middle and junior high school grades will require teachers with more sophisticated backgrounds to enable them to help students investigate and explore the world of work and to begin the process of vocational orientation. This may call for an occupational teacher with specialized training for teaching about occupations, but not for teaching *an* occupation. The senior high schools will need teachers who can work intensively with maturing students to help them narrow down their vocational choices and plan their career goals while still keeping their options open. For some there may be need for still other occupational teachers who can help them learn in more depth the skills and knowledges of a cluster of related occupations, so that they can gain entry to one of them if they choose, or move on to post high school education for further preparation.

Under such a plan, occupational teachers would need to develop different degrees of occupational skill and skill specialization, depending upon the level of service and the instructional role which they will fill. Only those at the post high school level would need the amount of skill development which is now so often demanded for teaching in the secondary schools. Teachers with this degree of occupational proficiency are in reality overtrained and overexperienced for the vocational maturity level of high school age students and for the objectives which can be defended in a high school program.

Teachers without full professional training but having the necessary work skills can be used effectively in manpower training programs and as part-time or periodic supplementary instructors for the upgrading of employed workers. They can also be brought in as resource people, consultants and demonstrators to supplement the work of the full-time certified teachers. Other areas of education are beginning to use differentiated staffing in various forms of team teaching and as resource specialists, and there is no reason why vocational education should not adopt some of the same methods.

New Approaches to Vocational Teacher Education

Only recently has any attention been directed toward ways of preparing vocational industrial teachers other than by recruiting them directly from industry, and most of these have involved only changes in the pedagogy employed after such teachers have been recruited. Cotrell and Miller, in a research project under the auspices of the Center for Research and Leadership Development for Vocational Education at the Ohio State University have explored the theory that there are elements of teaching techniques which are common to the teaching of all occupations and which can be identified by analysis and developed into an instructural model.[7] *Micro-teaching* (learning to teach using a very small group of students), a technique borrowed from general teacher education, has been tried in a few vocational teacher education programs. Yet none of these so-called innovations introduce any fundamental change into the preparation of vocational teachers, but are really only new devices for carrying out a traditional process. What is needed is some really new process for producing the professional vocational teacher—a process which will avoid the need for trying to turn craftsmen into teachers.

Teachers of other subjects prepare themselves for their careers by choosing teaching as a vocation while they are in high school and then enrolling as a freshman in a collegiate institution which offers a teacher education program. In earning their degree they master the subject they will teach (their major), achieve a substantial liberal education and also receive the professional preparation needed for certification. Some students, of course, transfer into such programs from other institutions or from other curriculums in the same institution, with appropriate transfer of credits. An important difference between these teachers and the converted craftsman is their early commitment to teaching as a career. There is need for vocational industrial teachers to be prepared in programs having the same features.

A few beginnings have been made. Rutgers University, with support from the Ford Foundation, has initiated a program which meets many of these criteria. The Cooperative Occupational Pre-Teaching Experience Program (COPE) is now in its third year and has met with considerable success.[8] It differs from the older arrangements by recruiting, at the time of graduation, high school students who have an interest in teaching but no occupational experience and then providing a way in which they can achieve both, together with a strong liberal education and a degree. Interested high school seniors are interviewed, screened and tested to determine their potential as future teachers. They are then placed by the university with an appropriate employer who agrees to share in the preparation of the young person for teaching by helping him learn the occupation he will teach. The student continues to work throughout his program and his work experience is supervised jointly by the employer and the university staff. At the same time he enrolls in the University College for a program of evening courses which include liberal studies, some occupationally related courses and professional education courses. When he has completed 5000 hours of work experience he may take a competency examination in his occupational specialty and if successful he is credited with 12 semester hours toward his degree. By following this program the degree can be earned in six years.

The plan has several advantages over the traditional method of securing vocational industrial teachers. It opens a career teaching opportunity to young people of the same age and education as those who prepare for teaching any other subject. It provides for subject matter competence, for a balanced education, for essential professional knowledge and skills, and it leads to a degree. The student knows that he is preparing for a career in teaching, not in industry.

There is no reason why such a plan could not be modified so that it would offer full-time rather than part-time study, with the occupational skills learned in carefully supervised cooperative work experience in shop, office, clinic or other appropriate work place. This experience would carry academic credit, and it could involve fewer hours but be even more varied than under the COPE plan. The quality and comprehensiveness of such experience is more important to the future teacher than its length. In this way the program could be completed and the degree earned within the usual four-year collegiate period. There would seem to be no limit to the number of occupational specialties that could be provided for under such a plan. Teachers of technical subjects could be prepared under this program and a fifth year, to include advanced practical experience and technical studies and leading to a master's degree could be developed for those planning to teach in community colleges and other post high school programs. This would also permit vocational teachers to share most of their preparation for teaching, not only with other vocational teachers, but with teachers of academic subjects as well. It would do much to break down the wall of separation which is still all too evident between these groups.

Leadership For Occupational Education

The sources of leadership for occupational education have historically been quite limited because there has been official exclusion of many potentially good leaders from leadership opportunities. They have been excluded for failure to meet certain narrow and rigid qualifications which have been sanctioned by tradition as being essential and for which no other experience or training could be substituted. Like many other traditions in vocational education these qualifications stem from the so-called service category basis for organizing and administering the program which originated with the Smith-Hughes law. The service categories have been identified as the federally funded areas of homemaking, agriculture and trade and industrial education. By making all occupations below the baccalaureate degree level eligible for funding it was the intent of Congress in passing the Vocational Education Act of 1963 to eliminate these categories as the organizational framework of the program. This was further emphasized in drafting the 1968 Amendments Act. Nevertheless, strong forces within the movement have resisted this change, and still insist on respecting the earlier occupational category approach. Since business education was not funded until 1963, and because the vocational status of homemaking was ambiguous, these two members of the vocational family, together with industrial arts, have been tacitly eliminated as sources for providing administrative leadership. This left in the potential leadership pool only persons associated with agricultural and trade and industrial education. Specialists from these two groups have consistently dominated the ranks of the status leaders at state and local levels.

Actually, most local programs of vocational education have not been, in reality, programs of vocational education at all. They have been either programs of agricultural education in the rural areas or programs of trade and industrial education in the cities, and more recently in the area vocational schools. The few courses which do not fit these categories, such as nursing, food services and cosmetology are appended to the more numerous trade type courses, and the administrator is nearly always a product of the trade and industrial program. Educators with backgrounds in business education, homemaking, industrial arts, and of course general education have in most states, by regulation or by interpretation of regulation, been ineligible for certification as administrators or leaders in occupational education.

Although some exceptions to this pattern have recently appeared in a few places, there is still a great reluctance to accept into leadership posts in vocational education anyone who has not been identified with one of the traditional service categories. This has brought about a crisis in leadership in occupational education. It is suffering not only from a numerical shortage of administrators and leaders, but more importantly from a lack of fresh thinking and innovative practice caused by excessive professional inbreeding. The 1967 Advisory Council on Vocational Education discovered this during the course of its study and reported that "there has been little attempt to bring personnel representing other disciplines into administrative positions at any level."[9]

The Need For a New Breed of Leadership

As in other social institutions, leadership philosophies and controlling policies in occupational education which were well suited and valid during one era are not necessarily defensible in another. It does no dishonor to respected leaders of the past to suggest that future leaders cannot and should not be bound by the decisions and the directions which they found it necessary to take. The founding fathers of vocational education were themselves never bound by tradition, and were they faced by the greatly different world which exists today they would not hesitate to make the changes which it demands. Occupational education can no longer afford to maintain a closed system in its leadership ranks. It must now tap many other sources of leadership than just those who are the products of its own programs and its own history if its leadership needs are to be met.

Tomlinson suggests that vocational education is now being served by a third generation of leaders. The first generation were the founding fathers who established the need and brought the program into existence. They were followed by a second generation, beginning about 1930, whose careers were spent largely in perfecting the administrative patterns needed to carry out the programs established by their predecessors. The present generation of leaders, he believes, are now in the adolescent stage of their careers, with fewer loyalties to tradition and to the past.[10] If this is correct, there may yet be time for the present leadership to make the changes which are urgently needed and which have yet to appear, but few of them have shown much of a tendency to do so. It is easier to follow old pathways than to pioneer new ones, even when the old pathways lead backwards.

A persistent official and quasi-official dogma of vocational education has been that no one can provide adequate leadership for it unless he has had work experience in an industrial, technical, agricultural or similar occupation. The rationale for this is hazy and difficult to understand. It has usually been defended on the grounds that without a personal background in the world of work, the administrator cannot understand the needs of vocational students or teachers nor relate successfully to employers, labor leaders and others whose cooperation is necessary. No such fact has ever been demonstrated, and it has often been disproved, but the theory has nevertheless prevented many capable educators from contributing their leadership skills to the program of occupational education. It is a part of the folklore of an earlier period which should now be abandoned, as the movement enters a more mature phase of its development.

What kind of leadership is needed for the new kind of occupational education that the times demand? Primarily future leaders must be people of vision, familiar with the past history of the movement but unencumbered by excessive loyalty to it, broadly educated, and able to understand the place of occupational education in the larger context of American society and American education. They should be individuals with broad knowledge, capable of making the connection between the new world of technology and the new world of work. They must be drawn from all of the fields that are represented in occupational education itself, as well as from every other educational discipline. Whether they are labeled as vocational educators is not important if their professional interests attract them to this field and if they possess the intellectual breadth and the leadership potential to contribute to it. They need to learn whatever is necessary to relate to occupational education, but they must become generalists rather than specialists within it.

The Vocational Amendments Act of 1968 sets aside funds to be used for the training of leaders and already certain universities have been approved for programs leading to the doctorate, designed for future leaders in occupational education. It is to be hoped that they will break out of the restrictive molds which have too often characterized similar programs for preparing administrators and other leaders. These new programs should de-emphasize the jurisdictional differences between services and give only minor attention to the details of budgets, finance, legalisms, buildings, equipment and the minutiae of administrative management. They should instead concentrate upon preparing leaders who can deal with new goals, establish new relationships with education at large, and understand the great social and human issues of our times as they relate to educating for work. They should include a thorough grounding in social and philosophical foundations, occupational sociology, social psychology, political science, manpower economics and the fundamentals of research. These should be studied under the best scholars in these fields and in programs which enroll administrative trainees from other areas of education. Some studies should apply to the problems of occupational education alone, but there is nothing so different about the administration of occupational education as to make necessary a completely separate preparation for its leaders.

Summary

The recruitment and preparation of teachers and leaders for occupational education has always presented problems in staffing its programs. Two traditions in particular have made it difficult to use the same means for teacher education that are followed in preparing teachers of other subjects. One of these is the demand for substantial occupational experience as a prerequisite for vocational teaching, and the other is the conviction that vocational education differs so much from all other forms of education that its personnel must be trained separately. In attempting to meet both these conditions a variety of ways has been used to prepare teachers for the several special service areas that have been created. In several subject areas the usual collegiate pattern leading to a degree has been followed, with the needed occupational skills taught as a part of the curriculum. Such teachers qualify with a minimum of occupational experience or none at all. For preparing trade and industrial teachers this plan has been rejected in favor of selecting experienced craftsmen and qualifying them as teachers by instructing them in basic pedagogical theory. This leaves them without college training and without a degree. It has resulted in serious problems of professional status and has encouraged the separation of vocational education from education as a whole.

Knowledge of an occupation is essential in order to teach it, but it has not been established that lengthy work experience is the only way to acquire it. If sufficient subject matter mastery can be gained in some occupations, such as business, by systematic study in a college program, it should be possible to accomplish it in all areas. The depth and breadth of occupational knowledge and the amount of skill proficiency required of teachers varies with the goals of their program and the maturity of their students. Long exposure to the occupation by the teacher is less important than a good knowledge of it coupled with the other qualities of a professional teacher. Many teachers will have to be prepared to teach about occupations, not how to practice them, to younger students. All vocational teachers need a well-balanced education, with a strong component of general liberal education, in addition to their technical studies, if they are to become educators rather than job trainers.

New, cooperative type programs for preparing all vocational teachers need to be established in colleges and universities. These programs should include a complete liberal education, together with strong professional preparation and, in addition, carefully planned and supervised off-campus work experience in the occupation to be taught. Occupationally related technical studies should also be a part of the curriculum. Young people should be recruited into such programs directly from high school, as they are now for teaching academic subjects. Many could also enter by transfer from the occupational curriculums of the two-year colleges, or in some cases after some full-time work experience.

Large numbers of administrators, curriculum workers and researchers, in addition to teachers will be needed for the growing demands of occupational education. Many of these should be attracted from other disciplines. The theory that only those who have had personal occupational experience and prior identification with vocational education can give effective leadership to its programs cannot be verified, and it is not supported by experience. Other leadership should be sought among vocational teachers, including those in all the occupational specialties. Advanced training at the doctoral level should be available for those who have the capacity to pursue it. It should be of the broadest possible character and should be coupled with similar programs designed to prepare general administrators and other educational leaders. It should avoid the minutiae of educational management and concentrate upon the broad understandings of society and of education which are so essential for educational leaders of the future.

REFERENCES

1. Cotrell, C. J., and Miller, A. J. "Design for Developing a Model Curriculum for Teacher Education." *American Vocational Journal* 44, no. 6 (September, 1969): 25.
2. U. S. Congress. *Vocational Amendments Act of 1968.*
3. Sinclair, W. "Certification of Vocational Teachers for Working With the Disadvantaged." Mimeographed. Trenton, New Jersey: Office of Teacher Certification and Education, New Jersey Department of Education, 1970.
4. Venn. *Man, Education and Work.*
5. COPE. *Third Annual Report of COPE.* New Brunswick: University College, Rutgers University (May, 1970).
6. Scobey, Mary M. *Teaching Children About Technology.* Bloomington, Ill.: McKnight and McKnight Co., 1968.
7. Cotrell and Miller. "Design for Developing a Model Curriculum for Teacher Education." *American Vocational Journal.*
8. COPE. *Third Annual Report of COPE.*
9. Tomlinson, R. M. "Implications (and Reflections on) the Vocational Education Amendments Act of 1968." *Journal of Industrial Teacher Education* (Summer, 1970).
10. Advisory Council on Vocational Education. *Vocational Education: The Bridge Between Man and His Work.*

CHAPTER 11

OCCUPATIONAL EDUCATION AND NATIONAL MANPOWER POLICY

Vocational Education as an Economic Asset

In Chapter 1 we found that one of the early goals of vocational education was to assure the nation of a reliable supply of trained manpower for its farms, factories and offices, and to keep its economy strong. This was one of the merits of the program that most appealed to the members of Congress and that greatly aided the effort to secure federal funding which came with the Smith-Hughes law. It has continued to be cited by the advocates of vocational education in and out of Congress as a reason for providing more public support. There is indeed impressive evidence of its contributions to the manpower needs of the nation. There have been tremendous advances in American agriculture, where an incredible record of technically proficient manpower preparation has enabled the nation to be well fed, and to export large surpluses of food, using less than ten percent of the manpower that was formerly required. This accomplishment is directly traceable to the impact of agricultural education, coupled with research. The training of skilled industrial and technical workers has helped to account for many of the gains in this vital segment of the economy. It has helped to win two world wars, and during World War II more than seven million production and supervisory workers were trained in the War Industries Training Program conducted in the public schools.[1] Yet when the nation is not at war the extent to which vocational education is relied upon by government and by employers for essential workers diminishes, and it is difficult to assess. It varies with the locality, the quality of the program, and with the economic climate. It is clear that up to this time only a very small fraction of the work force has had the benefit of vocational education in the schools.

Manpower Planning and National Needs

At the close of World War II, and with the memory of the 1930 depression years still fresh, there was much fear of renewed unemployment as the nation moved from a wartime to a peacetime economy. Government responded to these fears by passing the Employment Act of 1946, by increasing support to public school vocational education through the George-Barden Act,[2] and by strengthening the federal and state agencies which dealt with manpower. The emphasis was upon the prevention or alleviation of unemployment more than upon the training of workers to meet employers' needs. The Employment Act of 1946 established for the first time a policy that makes government responsible for full employment and for overall manpower planning, and it requires the President to report annually to Congress and the nation on the state of manpower affairs and needs. The overall planning, however, has failed to take place.

Fortunately, no widespread unemployment developed after the war, but rather a period of economic growth and general prosperity. Then, during the late 1950s, the fear of technical and military advantage over the United States by the Soviet Union was aroused in this country when the first space satellite was launched by the Soviets. This quickly led to the passage of the National Defense Education Act.[3] This law used the need for military and scientific defense capability as a basis for increasing financial support to certain areas of education, including the education of highly skilled technicians. The technical manpower resources of the United States were quickly mobilized, and within ten years we had not only caught up with the Soviets but far surpassed them in space accomplishments. It is good to recognize that this was done by workers who were the earlier products of the American school system, and that the schools were producing this trained manpower long before the appearance of Sputnik—an event which brought much criticism of the alleged failure of the public schools to equal Soviet educational attainments.

During the decade of the 1960s a whole series of laws relating to national manpower needs were enacted by Congress. The Manpower Development and Training Act of 1962[4] was followed by the Vocational Education Act of 1963, the Economic Opportunity Act of 1964,[5] the Appalachian Regional Development Act of 1965,[6] the Public Works and Economic Development Act of 1965,[7] and the Vocational Education Amendments Act of 1968.[8] In all of this legislation, however, the major emphasis had changed from that of satisfying the nation's need for trained manpower to the reduction of unemployment through education and training—in other words, from the needs of the nation to the needs of the individual. This change was greatly influenced by the growing awareness that even in this period of high economic activity there remained large pockets of unemployment among youth and among the disadvantaged, as the discussion in Chapter 8 revealed.

This list does not include several major pieces of legislation supporting general elementary and secondary education and adult education which were passed during the same years and which, in our technological society, are as vital to producing skilled manpower as are laws bearing the manpower label. Within the same period, the existing program for the vocational rehabilitation of the handicapped, another manpower program, was expanded and financially strengthened. During that time also, the Federal-State network of Employment Service Centers was given additional funding, personnel and responsibilities.

Thus, since World War II, the United States has had an uncertain policy with respect to its manpower problems, fluctuating in priorities from the need of employers for workers to national defense needs, to the need for jobs for the unemployed to reduce social unrest. In addition, the policy has been piecemeal in character, with legislation created in response to current needs as they arose, with responsibilities divided among numerous agencies of government, and without consistent or long-term goals. Furthermore, there has been little coordination and much competition between the various systems which have been called upon to deliver manpower services.[9]

The Fragmentation of Manpower Effort

One reason for the multiplicity of agencies engaged in manpower activities is the long standing jurisdictional rivalry among various agencies at federal, state and local levels, with each struggling to increase its power, prestige and personnel. Federal and state departments of labor have always felt that the training of workers was a function more nearly related to their particular domain than to the purposes of the public schools. As an expression of this feeling the Bureau of Apprentice Training was established in the Department of Labor in 1937, with corresponding units in the state departments of labor.[10] Its scope was later widened to include other forms of worker training, and when the Manpower Training and Development Act was passed in 1962, state and federal Departments of Labor were assigned equal authority with the U. S. Office of Education in the administration and operation of programs. The Department of Labor had made a strong effort to become the sole administrative agency for this program. The United States Department of Labor has responsibility for the interests of all workers, but in reality it serves largely as an arm of organized labor, and this is also true at the state level. Labor has much influence in Congress and in state legislatures, and there has always been some degree of contest between labor interests and vocational educators for the favor of legislators and legislation. Organized labor has never given enthusiastic support to the program of vocational education in the schools, partly because of its competitive interest in the training of workers and partly because of its desire to avoid an oversupply of skilled people.

In recent years similar competition in job training activities has arisen between public vocational education and the programs directed by the Office of Economic Opportunity and the many local community action groups financed through anti-poverty legislation. As a result there has been little cooperation and much duplication among the many local activities designed to prepare the disadvantaged for employment. Needless to say, political considerations and the necessity for respecting the political power of various groups have contributed to this fragmentation of effort. A number of attempts to set up coordinating structures in each locality in order to reduce the duplication of services have generally met with little success.

Aside from the need to respond to the claims of the competing groups for a share in manpower training, the Congress has never been disposed to depend upon vocational education in the public schools as the chief source of trained manpower, or, for that matter, to assign the responsibility for manpower development to any single agency. In the 1930s several non-school agencies, such as the National Youth Administration, the Civilian Conservation Corps, numerous collegiate educational programs, and the Bureau of Apprentice Training were created for purposes of education and work training. During World War II, when all resources for training were mobilized, four manpower training agencies were authorized and funded in addition to the War Industries Training Program in the public schools. These were the Bureau of Apprentice Training, the National Youth Administration, the Training Within Industry Program, and the Higher Education Defense Training Program. They operated independently and sometimes competitively until late in the war when they were all placed under the administration of the War Manpower Commission, an umbrella agency, together with the United States Employment Service. This Commission was also authorized to assign workers to essential jobs and to control job changing by workers. It went out of existence with the end of the war but the brief period of its operation was probably the only time in our history that there has been a unified national manpower policy affecting the civilian work force. Yet the powers which this agency exercised were so sweeping that they could never be tolerated except during a time of grave national emergency.[11]

Local, Regional and National Needs

In time of war the national welfare can properly claim priority over regional, local or individual needs, but at all other times these needs, and the privileges they imply, have to be considered in a free society. Manpower policies in a free labor market, and in a pluralistic society embracing many group and individual interests, must be flexible enough to accommodate all of them.

The program of occupational education in the public schools has long been federally influenced, state dominated, but locally oriented. The technique most often used to determine the occupations to be taught and the numbers to be trained has been the community survey—a device which is still employed for program planning. Many local programs in communities having only a few industries have geared their programs almost exclusively to the employment needs of their own community, and have become, in effect, vestibule schools for local employers. On the other hand, as the need for farm workers has continued to decrease most young people who are raised on farms will be unable to find employment there and they must migrate to localities where non-farm jobs are available. Yet the program of vocational education in the rural schools has not generally diversified its offerings to prepare them for other occupations. Little thought has been given to the needs or trends of the regional, state or national labor market in planning most programs of vocational education in the past, and the extent to which this will be done in the future is still uncertain.

Vocational Education and Manpower Planning

The Vocational Education Act of 1963 and the 1968 Amendments Act stress that the education to be offered must be "realistic in the light of actual or anticipated opportunities for actual employment." The Manpower Development and Training Act does not permit any training to be started unless the Employment Service first conducts a survey and certifies that there is a need for those who will be trained, and that they will have reasonable probability of employment. This requirement for matching the occupations to be taught and the numbers to be trained with the demands of the labor market has caused the administrators of the Vocational Education Acts to require from the states one-year and five-year projections of their programs, based upon a labor demand-supply analysis in each state. In theory this would keep manpower supply related more closely to manpower needs. It is also intended that programs that are approved shall be reviewed at the end of each planning period to learn how well the goals have been met.

However desirable such planning and accounting may be in theory, whether it is a practical procedure is open to question. In reality it may break down under the weight of bureaucratic delay and the sheer difficulty of the task. With the limited means of data gathering and the incomplete knowledge of manpower variables now available to us it is impossible to predict manpower needs in detail with any degree of certainty. In most cases employers simply do not know what their needs for workers will be five years hence, and often not even 'one year in advance. The economy and the labor market in a modern technological nation is too vast, too complex and too variable to enable anyone to graph or chart it much in advance. Even the Soviets, with power to control employment policy and to manipulate manpower at will, met with failure in attempting to deal with their economy in this way. Changing public attitudes on major issues, translated into public policy through political response, can, in our system, quickly shift the requirements of large sections of the economy. The current strong de-emphasis upon space exploration and defense spending, coupled with a sudden national concern for pollution control illustrates very well how a large segment of trained manpower in one industry and one geographic area can become surplus while the demand for skills of quite another kind builds up in another.

The fact that there are so many inputs into the labor force, of which vocational education is but one, further complicates the attempt to plan programs upon the projected demands of the labor market. The kinds of non-school sources of labor market supply and the numbers they contribute cannot be even approximately known to the vocational planners, nor to anyone else, because they depend upon millions of individual decisions, unknown in advance. In any case, educators are not trained as economists or economic analysts, and until many more of them have some training in this field they will even be unable to communicate with the specialists who are. To review and monitor the program plans of vocational educators in thousands of local centers by some central authority would require federal and state bureaucracies so large as to defeat their own purpose, and might bring the entire process to a standstill.

The techniques of community manpower surveys which were useful in earlier times are now of doubtful validity or value. Not only do they fail to reveal a very clear picture of existing manpower distribution but they are quite inadequate for projecting future needs. Even the most elaborate and costly surveys of this type are unable to identify and quantify satisfactorily the kinds of workers that the future labor market will require and that employers will buy. At the present time no agency has the know-how or the personnel with which to do this. Therefore, trying to plan vocational education on the demand-supply basis is rather futile if the attempt is made to translate such projections into numbers required for discrete occupations. Estimates of future demand cannot be made except in the broadest of terms, and even then with considerable risk of error. This is another reason for organizing vocational curriculums around broad clusters of occupations, so that the individual has many options in a fluctuating labor market. The greater his specialization the greater the risk of skill obsolescence and unemployment.

New Attempts at Manpower Planning

The piecemeal character of manpower policy and the proliferation of training agencies and functions has led recently to attempts by government to consolidate and streamline the many manpower programs.[12] Legislation to accomplish this was introduced in the Congress in 1969 in the form of three different bills.[13, 14, 15] All of these proposals are aimed at assisting the unemployed to find jobs and they include such measures as counseling, education, training, placement, relocation and a centralized, computerized job bank. They are designed to help the disadvantaged and others who have been thrown onto the job market by the schools, but have not been prepared for work or provided with employment. They would apparently supersede the present Manpower Development and Training programs. At any rate, as proposed in this legislation, educators would have little connection with the programs to be authorized, since administration would be in the Department of Labor and with political officials of local communities dealing directly with Washington.

It is difficult to know how the Congress views public education and its role in relation to these new manpower proposals. The fact that there are continuous efforts to change existing manpower legislation seems to indicate congressional dissatisfaction with what is being accomplished under present programs, for the funding requested for the new programs far exceeds the amounts authorized for vocational education. These new manpower proposals once again place the emphasis upon rescuing the educational casualties of society, rather than preventing these casualties through a reformed and functional system of occupational education in the schools. Yet it is generally acknowledged that unless the stream of undereducated and unemployable youth coming forth from the schools can be dried up, efforts to undo the harm they have suffered through welfare oriented programs of work training will continue to be inefficient, largely ineffective, and never ending.[16]

The Schools and Manpower Policy

The question is not whether the schools should become involved in manpower policy—they *are* involved in it. Education is the largest single contributor to a trained and competent labor force. It can modestly but rightfully claim the largest share of the credit for the technological pre-eminence enjoyed by this nation, because it has not only produced the educated work force but also the educated and skilled management without which capital and natural resources would stagnate.[17] Therefore, to ignore the further potential of education, and especially occupational education in meeting present and future manpower requirements would seem to be extremely shortsighted. Yet at the present time the nation and its leaders seem to be floundering in their efforts to arrive at a rational policy for the development and conservation of the human resources represented by the nation's manpower.

If we are to maintain the diversity of opportunities and the freedom to choose which have been the cornerstone of American life and enterprise, no monolithic or overly centralized approach to manpower policy can be accepted. Nevertheless there is clear need for some coordination of effort and some consolidation of services, and most important, for agreement upon goals and roles. The public schools cannot become the sole agency for developing the nation's manpower, although there is no other agency with such long experience or as great a potential for providing the indispensable foundations for such development. By modernizing its programs of general education and by introducing an updated program of occupational education which is not a replica of 1920, the schools can play a powerful role in preparing all our citizens for productive and satisfying work. They cannot accept the full responsibility for meeting all manpower needs. They cannot create jobs. They cannot assure full employment, make all work creative, or guarantee decent wages for all, although an enlightened program of occupational education can contribute to these kinds of goals. Other institutions in our society, other agencies of government, and other social and economic decision makers will have to share in combating the social ills of unemployment, poverty, and economic insecurity. A manpower policy that is not supported by other, related public policies is no policy at all. Education and training alone are not enough. Without changes in other areas they can only produce the best trained and educated unemployed in the world.

Perhaps the most insightful statement of the relation of occupational education to the manpower policies of the nation to appear in recent years is found in the 1968 report of the Advisory Council on Vocational Education. It says,

> The objective of vocational education should be the development of the individual, not the needs of the labor market. One of the functions of an economic system is to structure incentives in such a way that individuals will freely choose to accomplish the tasks which need to be done. Preparation for employment should be flexible and capable of adapting the system to the individual's need rather than the reverse. The system for occupational preparation should supply a salable skill at any terminal point chosen by the individual, yet no doors should be closed to future progress and development.[18]

Summary

Occupational education in the public schools has been supported by federal funds since 1917, although the level of funding has never been really generous. Justifications for its continued support as one of the nation's manpower resources have included the need for trained workers, the urgencies of national defense, and the need to combat unemployment and help the handicapped and the disadvantaged. One or another of these purposes has had priority at different times, depending upon shifting public concerns, and for the most part the program of vocational education has served the nation well in trying to achieve them.

The nation has never had, and does not now have, a well defined, consistent policy with respect to manpower development. At the national level the problem has been dealt with piecemeal by specialized legislation, with each new law enacted to deal with a new social crisis. The issue of manpower policy is a very complex one, with many interacting forces involved, and to a large extent the relationships between them have been lost sight of in the effort to cope separately with each situation as it arises. The 1960s saw an unusually large amount of legislation enacted dealing with manpower questions, but no fundamental or integrating philosophy emerged to relate the numerous laws.

Manpower decisions and activities are now spread among a great many different agencies, each of which acts independently. Proponents of vocational education in the public schools would like to have their program become the heart of the manpower development system for the nation, because they believe that education, rather than skill training alone, is what undergirds the manpower effectiveness of the American people. However, rivalry and jurisdictional interests among agencies are probably too strong to permit this to happen. There is also a serious question as to whether any single agency can perform this role.

Vocational educators and other training agencies have relied upon the labor demand-supply theory in planning their programs. It is beginning to appear that our technologically based economy is now too complex and too rapid in its changes to permit the continuous monitoring of the need for workers and the prediction of training needs which this theory requires. In a society where the decisions as to what jobs are to be offered and who wishes to accept them are made freely by employers and workers, the possibility of anticipating these decisions by educational planners is remote. This would suggest that preparation for work life should be offered in the broadest possible terms, so that the individual is left with as many options as possible. Devices such as a national computerized job vacancy bank may be of some assistance in identifying available jobs, but they cannot take account of the worker's willingness to change locations, nor of the multitude of other human variables which cannot be programmed.

Manpower policies tend to concern themselves with assuring a sufficient and properly balanced supply of workers and with matching people to jobs. Education, on the other hand, must place first priority on the needs of the individual for a satisfying work life rather than upon the needs of the labor market.

REFERENCES

1. Prosser, Charles; Hawkins, Layton; and Wright, J. C. *Development of Vocational Education.* Chicago: American Technical Society, 1951.
2. U. S. Congress. *Vocational Education Act of 1946.* Public Law 586, 79th Cong., 1946.
3. U. S. Congress. *National Defense Education Act.* Public Law 85-864, 85th Cong., 1958.
4. U. S. Congress. *Manpower Development and Training Act of 1962.*
5. U. S. Congress. *Economic Opportunity Act of 1964.*
6. U. S. Congress. *Appalachian Regional Development Act of 1965.* Public Law 89-4, 89th Cong., 1965.
7. U. S. Congress. *Public Works and Economic Development Act of 1965.* Public Law 89-136, 89th Cong., 1965.
8. U. S. Congress. *Vocational Education Amendments Act.*
9. Venn. *Man, Education and Manpower.*
10. U. S. Congress. *Fitzgerald Act of 1937.* Public Law 308, 75th Cong., 1937.
11. U. S. Congress. *War Manpower Legislation, 1942-1943.*
12. Venn. *Man, Education and Manpower.*
13. U. S. Congress. *The Comprehensive Manpower Training Act.* 91st Cong., 1969.
14. Ibid.
15. Ibid.
16. Venn. *Man, Education and Manpower.*
17. Drucker, Peter. *Technology, Management and Society.* New York: Harper and Row, 1970.
18. Advisory Council on Vocational Education. *Vocational Education: The Bridge Between Man and His Work.*

CHAPTER 12

THE COMING OF AGE OF VOCATIONAL EDUCATION

Two Worlds

The history of vocational education straddles two worlds. It began in the relatively stable, relatively simple and largely rural world of 1917, but it finds itself today in the complex, urbanized, unstable and technologically dominated world of the late twentieth century. If not in all respects, at least in many, the distance between these two worlds is as great as that between the Renaissance man of the fifteenth century and the cave man. To bridge this gap and to adjust to the realities of today's world is a difficult task for any of our institutions. It is especially difficult for education, the institution which has been created to maintain the threads of culture, learning and discovery through the changing generations, and which is more oriented toward stability than toward change. There are signs that education is faltering, and we cannot be as hopeful about its future as we used to be. To add to the difficulty, most of the changes which have occurred have come within the short space of the last thirty years. John Gardner speaks about the normal processes of institutional decay and thus the need for the constant renewal and revitalization of social institutions. The question is whether education, including vocational education, can respond to this need and respond soon enough.

Vocational education in America was born into a world where nearly half the people lived and worked on farms. Most of the rest were employed in industry. The cities existed, and some of them were large, but the great rural-urban migration had yet to come. Industrialization had arrived, but a great deal of the heavy manual labor was still performed by human hands and backs. It required the great majority of the work force just to produce the basic essentials of life—food, clothing and shelter. An eighth-grade education was considered to be a good education, and many, probably most, young people entered the world of work with less. High school graduation was accomplished by a very few, and fewer than ten percent of these went on to college. It was a time when Benjamin Franklin's observation that "he who has a trade has an estate" was literally true, because the skilled worker could be reasonably sure of employment wherever he went. It was a time when an occupation learned in youth would assure a livelihood for as long as a man wished to work, because technological change came too slowly to threaten the value of his skills during a normal lifetime. The effects of science and technology had begun to be felt, but not for many years would they surge forward to dominate life and work as they do today.

Today the world is vastly different. Less than five percent of our workers are engaged in farming. Two thirds of the nation's workers produce no food, clothing or shelter, for they work in service occupations. Only in a high technology economy could this be possible. Heavy manual labor has been all but eliminated from the work men do. Never before in history has technology brought the benefits which are now enjoyed in this society, by bringing relief from the age old burdens of hunger, disease, and heavy labor to the majority of a great population, with the ready potential of doing so for the rest. We are on the brink of nearly total automation of the means by which the necessities of life, and many luxuries, are produced.

To enter the adult world today with only an eighth-grade education is to be without hope of survival. Seventy-five percent of young Americans complete high school and forty percent of these go to college, and both figures are rising. During the thirteen years between 1949 and 1962, 2.2 million jobs requiring less than nine years of education disappeared from the economy. During the same years there was an increase of 3.3 million jobs calling for nine to twelve years of education, an increase of four million jobs calling for twelve to sixteen years of education, and an increase of four million jobs requiring sixteen or more years of education. This represents an educational upgrading of fourteen million jobs in thirteen years, and the trend has accelerated since.[1] Clearly, the future belongs to the educated.

A trade learned in youth no longer assures lasting economic security. Changes brought by technology may be so extensive that the occupation will be substantially altered, or even eliminated, and this may happen more than once during a working lifetime. Even those with an advanced education, if it is highly specialized, are not immune from such threats to their employment.

The world of 1917 was neither primitive nor easy, but thoughtful, educated men of that time could understand the meaning of its major problems. Now no one understands the full implications of technology and each specialist understands only his own specialty.

A Time For Transition

It is within this context that vocational education today must be examined and re-evaluated. When this is done it becomes apparent that as an institution it is badly in need of renewal and revitalization. The achievements of yesterday, however glorious, carry little weight today, and the old mandates have expired. Occupational education will now have to be re-directed in terms of today's realities and tomorrow's probabilities. As a part of the educational system, it has been understandably slow to change.[2]

Two recent studies, resulting in two landmark reports, have spelled out the changes that are needed. The first was the report of the 1962 Panel of Consultants, *Education for a Changing World of Work*, which resulted in the Vocational Education Act of 1963. This law required a formal review at the end of five years of the progress made under its provisions. This review was made by the ad hoc Advisory Council on Vocational Education which published its report in 1968, *Vocational Education—The Bridge Between Man and His Work*. It found that the progress toward the new goals set forth in the 1963 Act had been slight. It reiterated these goals and suggested additional changes, and these were accepted by the Congress and incorporated into the Vocational Education Amendments Act of 1968. Thus the way has been shown to the reforms that should take place in occupational education if it is to remain as a useful institution in American society, yet the changes have scarcely begun. There has been far more enthusiasm about constructing new buildings, buying new equipment, and enrolling additional pupils than about broadening the goals, changing organizational patterns, and planning the substantive curriculum revisions which the new legislation asks for. The result is the appearance of impressive new buildings, filled with the most modern and costly equipment, but designed for programs which often differ little from those of 1920.

A Time to Mature

Occupational education has passed through its childhood and has perhaps lingered too long in its adolescence. It must now come of age in a world which will not long tolerate institutions that cannot adapt and that continue to be geared to yesterday's conditions.

Those who can recall Washington Irving's tale of Rip Van Winkle may remember that on his way up to the mountain where he later fell asleep, Rip passed a tavern with a sign carrying a picture of King George the Third. On his way back home, after sleeping for twenty years, he passed the same tavern, but the picture on the sign was now that of George Washington. Rip had not only slept for twenty years, he had slept through a revolution. We too are in the midst of a revolution—a revolution created by science and technology, and no institution of society can afford to sleep, or even drowse through it. It is the greatest single force to affect the lives of men in modern history, and those that fall asleep can expect to be abandoned, as new ways to perform their functions are invented to replace them.[3]

One evidence of maturity is to be able to cope adequately with change, to respond intelligently to new conditions, and to minimize the insecurities that change brings. Adapting to change is not easy, either for individuals or institutions, and developments which bring the necessity for change always seem threatening to both. When the pace of change is swift the capacities of men to respond to it are severely tested, and the scientific-technological revolution of our age presents just such a test to us now. We cannot look forward to a slowdown in its impact, but, on the contrary we must be prepared for its continued acceleration.

If education has found it difficult to adjust to this new era in human affairs, vocational education has found it even more so. Occupational education, with its roots firmly planted in the early legislation from which it sprang, has clung tenaciously to the doctrines embodied in those laws, because this seemed to be the way to continuity and stability. It can no longer do so. It must relinquish some of the cherished theories of the past because they have been rendered invalid by new knowledge and by the conditions of modern life. New goals and new ways of achieving them must be formulated to replace them, and a doctrinaire approach is no longer possible.

Vocational education should not undertake these changes just for the sake of change, nor to satisfy the current fashion in education to appear innovative. The history of American education is replete with popular movements which have aroused great enthusiasm but, lacking sufficient research and pilot testing, have soon proved to have unforeseen weaknesses and have been quietly abandoned. The changes needed in vocational education are not superficial, but fundamental. They are changes dictated, not by questionable or untested theories, but by sweeping, documented changes in the nature of society itself.

Occupational Education For the Modern Age

If occupational education expects to serve the nation as well in the future as it has in the past it must be prepared to reorganize and redirect its efforts to coincide with the nature of the modern world. This book has attempted to identify the issues in occupational education which are most in need of critical review, and to marshal the best knowledge now available for examining them. As a result of examining these issues in this way, it is now possible to draw some basic conclusions as to the changes that are most urgently needed in occupational education in America's schools. They are these:

The organization and operation of the program of vocational education in terms of occupational categories must be abandoned.

This has already been accomplished in the most recent federal legislation, and in the latest administrative codes, but the program continues to operate as if this had not happened. Furthermore, as new programs are planned, the changes in the legislation and the codes are often disregarded. Chapter 1 described the strong influence of a social welfare philosophy among those who secured the passage of the Smith-Hughes law. This philosophy places the needs of individuals for improving their lot above the needs of employers for trained workers, yet when the Smith-Hughes law was drafted the needs of major occupational fields predominated, and the entire program was subsequently structured around occupational service categories. In the Vocational Education Act of 1963 the Congress purposely abandoned this approach, eliminated the service categories, and instead designed the law to meet the needs of different groups of people, so broadly defined as to include all Americans.

There was a practical, as well as a philosophical basis for this action. If vocational education is to be organized, administered and funded in terms of specific occupational categories, with new occupations added one by one by legislative amendment, the number of occupations, and therefore the number of people served must always remain small unless the whole program is to become a legal and administrative monstrosity. The seven service areas authorized under the Smith-Hughes, George-Barden and other legislation represented the practical limit to which this concept could be pushed and it is obvious that if occupational education is to expand to reach the multitude of unmet needs some other form of organization is necessary. What was once a rational and logical way to organize and administer vocational educational has now become a straitjacket. Congress therefore wiped out the service categories in favor of an open, flexible, unrestricted policy of organization and administration.

This change has not been accepted in practice. Although funding is no longer based upon occupational categories, but upon the kinds of people served, tradition insists upon retaining the organizational structure of the former. In one state, a lobby within the program, representing vocational agriculture, is now trying to force the creation, in the state education department, of an administrative position for vocational agriculture with a rank equivalent to the assistant superintendent for all secondary education in the state.[4]

To attempt to serve the future members of a labor market as complex, diversified and fast changing as our own by a program administered in behalf of discrete occupational categories is patently impossible. Unless the spirit, as well as the letter of the most recent federal legislation is accepted and followed, occupational education will never be able to meet the social goals which the nation set for it when this legislation was adopted.

Occupational education must accept broader goals and additional responsibilities. Occupational education must now recognize that it has the responsibility for assisting every citizen to know the world of work, to make a wise choice of his vocational direction, to prepare adequately for it, and to find success and satisfaction in his occupational life. Heretofore it has been concerned chiefly with but one of these goals. It must accept responsibility for *all* students in their career planning and decision making, including those whose decisions lead to preparation requiring higher education. It must be prepared to help people enter any occupation for which they can qualify. Its services must begin in the elementary school and continue through the post high school years.[5] These objectives are far different from those of training a few high school pupils to enter one of a few selected occupations.

Occupational education must depart from its tradition of separatism. Vocational education can never hope to measure up to the kinds of responsibilities which have just been suggested unless it can remove the barriers which keep it divided from the rest of American education. Its full membership into the educational family is long overdue, and American education has never been more ready for it. Only as a part of a unified system of public education can vocational education contribute fully to the education of all Americans. Only within such a system can Americans enjoy the rich resources which occupational education can bring to their schools.

Occupational education must learn to accept and profit from critical evaluation. One evidence of maturity is the capacity for constructive, critical self-evaluation and for rational rather than emotional reaction to honest evaluations made by others. Vocational education has shown little capacity for self-criticism.

The *Journal of Industrial Teacher Education* is a respected and well edited publication for professional workers in vocational education. From time to time its editors invite qualified vocational educators to contribute articles which give differing positions on topics of current importance in occupational education. In a recent issue of this kind the editor wrote that it was difficult to find contributors who would take a controversial position for fear of displeasure or reprisal by their superiors.[6]

Surely reprisals or reprimands used to suppress scholarly discussion are not the mark of professionalism. In a fully matured profession there can be no place for such attitudes, for they illustrate all too clearly the lack of critical capacity that professionalism demands.

This question is closely related to the recurring issue of the image of vocational education. This image is not enhanced among professional educators by reactions such as those just described. And if the public image of vocational education is less favorable than it should be, defensive and self-justifying attitudes will not correct it. It will require two things to change it. One is for occupational education to merge fully into the larger system of public education. The second is for its programs to achieve high quality in terms of the larger goals of American education—programs which are not in conflict with the legitimate aspirations of American parents for their children.

Occupational education must be more than a training program. Producing efficient workers for American employers can no longer be the prime objective of occupational education. It will be a useful by-product of a program which has much more comprehensive goals, but which places the educational needs of people above the immediate needs of the labor market. Employers do not expect the schools to produce workers who are tailored to any one of the vast number of job specialties that make up that labor market, and if this is what providing a salable skill is interpreted to mean, then vocational education faces a hopeless task. In attempting to do this, essential elements of a balanced education have been omitted from too many programs of vocational education in the past. Today's economy calls for a new kind of occupational curriculum which will provide a truly educational experience.

Specialized occupational preparation should be deferred until the post-high school period. This would still leave occupational education with a more prominent place in the high school than it has today, but with different objectives. During the high school years the program should concentrate upon vocational orientation, exploration, career planning and vocational decision making for all students. Specialized training in a particular occupation for most high school students is no longer compatible with technological-economic realities nor with societal norms. For those students whose vocational maturity may warrant it, a cluster or career development curriculum should be created, because the three track curriculum of academic, general and vocational education has not worked in the high school.[7] Until now, to have less than a high school education is to be undereducated. For the future, anyone whose education has not gone beyond high school will be undereducated. Too many outdated programs of occupational education are with us today because of yesterday's failure to foresee the extent to which schooling would be extended, and we should not be misled into inadequate planning for the future.

Occupational education should become one component in a comprehensive system of human resource development. This concept embraces more than just the objective of manpower development, which generally means only a system for assuring our private and public enterprises of sufficient numbers and kinds of competent workers. The development of human resources aims at the fulfillment of the individual, the full utilization of talent, and the greatest possible realization of all human potential. Occupational education can play a vital role in this process. It can form the linkage from childhood and youth to occupational life, and between school and the world of work. Only when viewed in this way does it become a form of education rather than a device for training workers.

Technology has a strong potential for de-personalizing and mechanizing the work life of men. It interposes the machine and systems of machines between man and his work, between man and his education, and between man and man. A pre-eminent task of education is to re-humanize man in an environment which tends to de-humanize him. The goal of education in a free society must be to produce informed, understanding, self-disciplined, socially responsible free minds in free men. As a means of human resource development, occupational education can lead toward this goal, but as only a form of training it never can.

Summary

All institutions of society have been deeply affected by the pervasive impact of the modern scientific-technological revolution. Education has had great difficulty in its attempts to adjust to these effects and to come to terms with the new world in which it finds itself. Occupational education has not yet been able to do so. Its philosophy and structure were appropriate for a world which was far different from the one in which it must now function. The nature of occupational life today, when the half life of technical knowledge is estimated to be ten years, has little resemblance to the world of work when vocational education began. Actually, one can scarcely think of any realm of American life in which the conditions today resemble those of 1917, yet occupational education has remained relatively unchanged since that time. It has not grown to the stage of maturity that the present times demand.

Occupational education is now faced with the necessity for coming of age through a process of philosophical growth and practical adaptation to the world as it now exists. It cannot depend upon past accomplishments to insure its future, nor upon traditional answers to problems which yesterday's world never anticipated. Some changes are so long overdue that the need for them is urgent. These are delineated in the report and recommendations of the Advisory Council on Vocational Education, published in 1968 and given official sanction by the Vocational Education Amendments Act of the same year. This Act should not be allowed to take on the character of sacred doctrine, as earlier legislation did, but must be thought of as pointing the way to continuous growth and change in a dynamic and responsive movement.

REFERENCES

1. United States Department of Labor. *Manpower Report of the President*. Washington, D. C.: Government Printing Office (March, 1963).
2. Coombs, Philip H. *The World Educational Crisis: A Systems Analysis*. New York: Oxford University Press, 1968.
3. Ellul, Jacques. *The Technological Society*. New York: Knopf, 1964.
4. Tomlinson, R. "Implications (And Reflections On) the Vocational Education Amendments Act of 1968." *Journal of Industrial Teacher Education*.
5. Feldman, M. "Vocational Education in a New Comprehensive System." *Today's Education* 57, no. 8 (November, 1969).
6. Suess, A. "Editorial Comment." *Journal of Industrial Teacher Education* (Summer, 1970).
7. Davies, Don. "Which Statistics Do You Read?" *American Vocational Journal* 45, no. 8 (November, 1970): 90-95.